*memories of Eric*

# Memories of
# Eric

EDITED BY GARY MORECAMBE
AND MARTIN STERLING

ANDRE DEUTSCH

# Foreword

Contained in this book are so many friends Eric and I made over the years. Many of those most dear to us are no longer here and are sorely missed. In particular, in 1999 we saw the passing of Ernie Wise, who had shared a forty-three-year partnership with Eric.

It is fascinating to read other people's memories of Eric, and to see him through their eyes.

Looking back on those years – the constant effort of touring to appear in variety theatres all over the country, the long summer seasons and Christmas pantomimes, the first tentative steps into the new medium of television – who could have foreseen the unprecedented success that was to follow for Eric and Ernie? A unique partnership. What staggers me is how it seems to have come and gone in a flash.

Eric and Ernie are now icons in this country. As a lasting tribute to Eric from his home town of Morecambe, in July 1999 we saw the unveiling of a statue on the sea-front performed by Her Majesty The Queen. Who would have thought – certainly, Eric didn't – that a young boy fishing on Morecambe sands with his Dad would one day be immortalized at that very spot?

I am sure this book will provide a further insight into the genius, and the man, my husband, Eric Morecambe.

Joan Morecambe
Hertfordshire, 1999

Eric and Joan,
1977

# Introduction

# Gary Morecambe

The older I get, the more tragic my father's death at the age of fifty-eight seems. Yet it is amazing how much he crammed into what can by today's expectations be regarded as a short life: the theatrical tours, the radio shows, the TV shows, the films – and it all began with such an unlikely, humble upbringing in the North of England.

Since his death in 1984, numerous are the times I have met people who either knew him or worked with him and are eager to pass on some little story – a telling moment – about the time they were in the company of Eric Morecambe.

By compiling this collection, my co-writer, Martin Sterling, and I will hopefully bring back many happy moments to those who have made generous contributions to this book, while simultaneously entertaining anyone who has ever enjoyed Eric's sense of humour.

What has been a particular revelation while working on this book is that something initially designed as light-hearted fun has in fact peeled back the layers of Eric, revealing the inner man in a surprisingly more candid way than any

biography to date – and I include in that statement Martin's and my own biographical effort.

My father was both a gentleman and gentle man, who always remained faithful to his talent and unpretentious about the many honours bestowed upon him. It was almost as though he came to regard his success as a great relief after the tough earlier years, rather than as an opportunity to wallow in new-found fame and fortune. At the very pinnacle of his success in the mid-1970s, he summed up his life's work in a few frank words which are typical of the man: 'Basically, what you see us doing with Morecambe and Wise on television is high-class rubbish.'

*Gary with his father, 1982*

What of my own memories of the great man? It is his sheer personality and eagerness to entertain his family and everyone else that spring most readily to mind. His own father, George, had been quite a chirpy character, prone to mischief and odd sayings. His mother, Sadie, who believed her only child had talent, did her bit by suggesting that Eric and Ernie team up as a double act.

I have no memories – not even one – of my father's practical role as a parent. He never cooked for us or bathed us, and our homework was beyond his own limited formal education. During my early years, he seemed to be away much of the time. It must have become increasingly difficult for him to slip back into domesticity. We learnt to accept his regular absences, and my mother went beyond the call of duty to compensate.

The question I was – still am – most often asked is 'What was it like having Eric Morecambe as your father?' It is a question that has, on occasion, even been posed by children of famous people. That somehow to me stresses the awe in which Eric is held. Having had but the one father, I have to say it was a relatively normal experience, though the use of the word 'relatively' suggests that life with such a man was never totally normal – it couldn't have been. Eric Morecambe is arguably the greatest postwar comedian this country has produced: a true one-off, a man who could generate instantaneous laughter unscripted.

He did his best to play the role of a normal parent – and succeeded for the most part – but that isn't quite the same thing.

The media, in particular the tabloid press, have often tried to make me appear the hard-done-by son who is bitter about his upbringing. One famous headline read something like 'HE MADE THE WORLD LAUGH, SO WHY DID HE MAKE MY LIFE A MISERY?'. Nothing could be further from the truth. My father was neglectful at times, irritating on occasion, but the mere fact that I would change nothing of what I experienced speaks volumes. I've always considered myself fortunate from the word go. I've had it both ways – the star parent, yet the normal upbringing – and there are certainly no angry words to be written to right any real or imagined wrongs. Life was and is great, and my world – maybe yours, too – is a quieter, sadder place without Eric Morecambe.

I suppose there were moments when I wished he was anything other than famous, but those moments were rare. Most of the anguish I experienced during my youth was at having to share him with his public, and that's something I now know my sister and brother also felt. He was instantly recognizable throughout Britain, and the professional within him made him feel obliged to deliver the whole Eric Morecambe rigmarole. He hated to let people down; hated them to think he was either not well or not funny. This made it difficult for him to have his quiet moments.

He dared not shut down completely. Even on holiday – especially on holiday – a part of him remained switched on. He reasoned that if he totally relaxed he might not be able – or want – to switch back on again.

One of the ironies concerning my father and Morecambe and Wise is that he never lost the fear that they might one day fail. It didn't haunt him on a daily basis, but it always lurked deep inside him, usually revealing itself in comments like 'You've got to be seen on TV to be a star. And you have to be a star.'

I agree with the late Roy Castle, who said that Eric had a serious side which he permanently suppressed. Whenever it began to show itself in too vociferous a manner, he would go quiet, almost afraid to be seen as anything but a clown.

The only difficulty in living with him was

The Morecambe family

that at times it was like living with a Morecambe and Wise show. That could be debilitating for the family and, also, for himself in the final analysis.

He was a man who saw everything in black and white. There were no grey areas. It was a notable failing, as most of his arguments were 'for' or 'against' and there was little room for compromise and debate. He wasn't a particularly volatile person, but his lack of tolerance sometimes gave that impression.

People often tell me how much I look like my father, and this I find genuinely flattering. However, I think our personalities are a little different. I see myself as the grey area to complement his black and white. Also, I know I couldn't have endured those years of boards-treading struggle – or, conversely, being the focus of attention – as he did, and look back on it all as having been wonderful. I've certainly never felt the urge to be a star, which to him was everything. Being a star meant all other aspects of his career were in working order, which is why Morecambe and Wise turned down so little during their long career. They thought it prudent continually to remind the public they were still there joking around.

Strange to say, I feel I didn't grow up, become my own person, until after my father had died. This is a feeling shared with

Michael Sellers (son of Peter) and Richard Olivier (son of Laurence). The son and his famous father are not conscious that they are both living in the giant shadow of that parent's fame – difficult enough to handle for the one who is famous, impossible for

the one upon whom the fame is merely an unrequested side-effect.

My final ascent into adulthood came when I moved my family to France in 1989. This was, in part, a deliberate move to escape everything associated with Eric Morecambe. It was a two-year breathing-space in which I had the opportunity to analyse what had been, and to understand what, if anything, had been the purpose of the long journey as the son of Eric Morecambe. It strikes me as paradoxical that it should all have culminated in a return to England in 1991 and my active involvement in Morecambe and Wise. Since then, I've had a bizarre and inexplicable desire to perpetuate and control Morecambe and Wise. I've become increasingly proud and defensive of them, and possibly an absolute bore on the subject.

I feel the greatest thing my father left his family is his popularity – the 'feel-good factor', as it's fashionable to call it. What was once no more than a satisfactory way of life for him is now a terrific testament to the talent of a very funny, lovable man.

As to anecdotes, I have chosen to kick things off with a handful of brief but vivid memories. There are, of course, hundreds I could have picked, but it is usually a specific handful which return to my mind every once in a while, and it is that which makes them worth recording.

☆

When I was about twelve, I was with my sister and parents staying with my paternal grandparents in Morecambe.

One evening, we went to visit relations nearby. My father and his mother, Sadie, had a close relationship based on ironic retorts and one-liners. It always seemed a bit aggressive to me, but that was just their way – perhaps the way of Northern families of that generation.

This particular evening, Sadie was going on about the wisdom of saving money. After a few minutes, my father had had enough of this and said, 'You know, you can't take it with you when you go. At least not where you're going – it'll only melt.'

☆

We were on one of our many summer holidays in Portugal, where my parents kept a villa.

Cilla Black and her husband, Bobbie, were regular visitors to the Algarve, and we met them one night at a beach-front restaurant called La Cigale. While we were waiting in the bar to be seated, we were approached by a woman who was well on the way to intoxication. She had recognized my father immediately and now seated herself on his lap.

'I know who you are,' she remarked in a bit of a slur. 'You're him. You're him.'

'If you want,' smiled my father.

'Oh, she's famous, too,' she said, suddenly noticing Cilla.

Then the woman picked up my father's

drink and sniffed the glass. 'Ugh! What are you drinking?'

Without a pause my father replied, 'That's very kind, I'll have a scotch and soda.'

To give her her due, she wasn't so gone as not to see the humour.

A few seconds later, the manager took her away.

Describing a friend who was trying to grow a beard for the first time, my father remarked, 'He looked like a slashed cinema seat.'

On the same subject – facial growth – he remarked to a bearded friend, 'Last time I saw anything like that on a face, the whole herd had to be destroyed.'

☆

I was going to watch an episode of a popular TV series back in the 1970s called *Night Gallery*. I decided I was too tired and would give it a miss. My father at once said, 'Then good night, Gallery.'

☆

My father walked into the house, having just returned from BBC Television Centre and a visit to the studio hairdresser.

'Hi, Dad,' I said, noticing the short back and sides. 'I like the haircut.'

'Good.'

'It makes you look like Sean Connery.'

'Yes. A very Shorn Connery.'

☆

At a drinks party, Eric was approached by a man who had met Eric's father, George, some years before.

'Tell me,' the man said awkwardly, 'is your father...er...is he...er...dead?'

'I hope so,' said Eric. 'We buried him.'

☆

As part of a promotional tour to launch my first book about my father, he and I went on *The Russell Harty Show*. During the on-air conversation I said to Russell that, with my father's second heart attack, I felt very much a part of it. My father dived in with, 'Yes – he caused it.'

End of any serious conversation.

Good reading.
G. M., Somerset, 1999

# Martin Sterling

I never met Eric – but that doesn't mean I didn't know him. My heroes when I was growing up were James Bond and Eric Morecambe. I notice my friend the actor Shaun Prendergast says the same thing in the second section of this book.

Maybe every lad growing up in a working-class family in the North during the sixties and seventies had the same two heroes, I don't know. What I do know is that I believed I had a personal link to Eric, so much so that I felt a tremendous sense of personal bereavement when he died. And that was shared with everyone else.

With all due respect to Tommy Cooper and Les Dawson (both of whom I adored) and to every other much-loved comedian no longer with us, were any of them mourned as much as Eric? I can't recall one who was. But why? What was there in Eric that made us love him so much?

I believe Eric was unique in that he touched everyone in a way that no other performer has ever managed and in a way that, perhaps, even he didn't understand. Everyone seemed to recognize instinctively that he was a genuinely decent human being. And he also had vulnerability. We all knew of his health problems, which is what gave his comedy, innocuous though much of it seemed on the surface, a dangerous edge. While we were laughing at one of his energetic dance routines, which of us didn't wonder guiltily whether he should be putting himself through that for our benefit?

I can trace my love for Eric Morecambe back to Christmas Day 1971. I was nine years old: the novelty of the new toys had long since worn off and boredom had set in. But then *The Morecambe and Wise Show* began. It was the one with Shirley Bassey getting the boot and an incredulous André Previn trying to conduct while Eric played 'all the right notes – but not necessarily in the right order'. An hour of television which is not simply classic but legendary. And it stopped me dead in my tracks.

Here, suddenly, was this extraordinary man who was doing this show for me. Just for me. Or at least, that's how it seemed. He wasn't a performer on television, he was a fellow conspirator, another schoolboy who just happened to look a bit older than my parents. We connected in a way I've connected with no other performer since. I remember looking round the room at my parents, my grandparents and my great-grandmother, and it was apparent to me, even at the age of nine, that he was connecting with them as well. Four generations of the same family and Eric meant the same to every person, literally from nine to ninety. For me, nothing has ever explained Eric's unique and enduring appeal more clearly than the memory of looking around our sitting-room that Christmas night.

The closest I ever got to Eric was when he and Ernie were arriving for a function at a hotel on Park Lane in 1983. I happened to be in London that day, and was passing when Eric arrived. Gary Morecambe and I have subsequently worked out that he was there, too: odd to think that five years later we would start working together.

Writing the biography of Eric and Ernie in 1994, and a play about Eric, both with Gary, has given me an insight into Eric Morecambe. And the more I learn about him, the more I like him. Isn't it wonderful to be able to say that?

Though I never met Eric, I have got to know his family well: his wife, Joan, and his children, Gail, Steven and, of course, Gary; I'm even godfather to his granddaughter, Dereka. Eric didn't only leave a wonderful legacy of laughter which we'll never stop enjoying; he also left a family who love, respect and admire him to this day. If that doesn't prove he was a damned good human being, as well as the British comic genius of the century, I don't know what does. But then you, like me, probably need no convincing.

M. S., Norfolk, 1999

# Part 1

# Family, friends and colleagues

# Sadie Bartholomew

Sadie Bartholomew was Eric's mother, and the following piece is
put together from things she said and wrote about her son over a
number of years. She died in 1977, seven years before Eric.

Eric has always claimed I pushed him into show business and he's even tried to sell me that idea. But that's not how I remember it. Eric loved performing and showbusiness practically from the time he could walk, which he did at nine months. We had a gramophone and he knew every record we possessed. He was like a little doll with a head of blond curls, and he soon learnt to speak.

Whenever we took him to relatives, all he wanted to do was perform. As soon as someone sat at the piano, you'd see a blond curly top no higher than the keyboard.

☆

He was a handful. I didn't dare leave the front door open, because he'd be off down the road. If I was taking him out, I found the best thing to do was to tie him by a scarf to the doorknob and let him sit on the step until I got ready. He had a little tam-o'-shanter with a pompom. I'd put it on his head, but he always pulled it off because he hated it.

One day he saw a kind-looking man coming down the street, and he said, 'Look, I've tied myself too tight. Can you let me go?' The unsuspecting man obliged and I came out to find the scarf hanging from the doorknob but no Eric.

I rushed to the bottom of Lancaster Road to look for him and saw two old men sitting on a bench.

'Have you seen a little boy go by?' I asked.

'Nay,' said one, 'but we've seen a little lass with a curly top carrying a tammy.'

'That's him,' I said. 'Did you see where he went?'

'There he is,' said the second man, pointing.

Eric was a little distance away, surrounded by a party of builders. They'd rigged up a plank on a couple of crates for him and Eric was going through his repertoire of nursery rhymes and more sophisticated numbers like 'I'm Dancing with Tears in My Eyes' and 'Blue Moon'. The tam-o'-shanter was his box office and he was doing very well. His audience was loving it.

Eric saw me and announced to his audience, 'That's me Mam, I'd better go now.'

One of the builders said to me, 'That little lad's a wonderful entertainer.'

Sadie and George Bartholomew with Eric, Gail and Gary, 1964

'I'll entertain *him* when I get home,' I replied.

'Well, folks,' Eric said to his audience, 'I'll have to be going now. See you tomorrow.'

'Over my dead body,' I said, dragging him away.

'It's been worth it,' Eric protested. 'Look at all these pennies. Has my Dad come home?'

'Wait till I get you home. You'll taste the strap.'

On the way back we stopped at a shop owned by a friend, Mrs Pascoe. I went in for a chat with her.

Eric went behind the counter and emerged with a dog lead. 'Better give me the strap now,' he said. 'It won't hurt so much with Mrs Pascoe watching.'

☆

Eric had a very happy childhood. Like all only children, he lacked the companionship of brothers and sisters, but he was never short of friends of his own age. And he had a wonderful relationship with his father. And, later, with Ernie, of course.

Eric was very temperamental, which I call sheer bad temper. When he and Ernie first started doing their double act, they often used to alter their gags. But if Ernie made a slip on the stage, Eric would go mad. 'You're not a bit of good, Ernie. You're meant to have learnt all this,' he'd say.

One day I got furious with him. 'Eric,' I said, 'don't you ever let me hear you speak to Ernie like that again. Go straight upstairs.'

When Eric had stomped up to his room, Ernie turned to me. 'You shouldn't have interfered, y'know,' he said quietly.

'But I was sticking up for you,' I said.

'Don't you see? Eric's only trying to make me the best feed in the business. And I'll tell you something else. He's going to be the best comic in the British Isles one day.'

Later, I told Eric what Ernie had said, and there was no more temperament from him again. Never another cross word, never any more argument. That's the honest truth.

Mother-in-law Alice, grandaughter Amelia and grandson Adam

Sadie and George, 1975

# Ernie Wise

The following thoughts from Ernie appeared in the programme of a show staged at the London Palladium by Thames Television, on 9 November 1984, as a tribute to Eric, six months after his death. Additional comments are from Ernie's autobiography, *Still On My Way To Hollywood* (Duckworth, 1990).

I first saw Eric give his audition for Jack Hylton in Manchester. He was wearing a black beret, bootlace tie, cut-down dress suit held together with a large safety pin, red socks, and holding a large lollipop. I thought it was ridiculous that anybody could walk about in the street dressed like that. He sang a song called 'I'm Not All There', then he did his impression of Flanagan and Allen but only did Allen. I've never been able to work that one out. No, we did not form the double act then; we had no idea of the future. We met later, in a show called *Youth Takes a Bow*, in which we both did single acts. I said, 'Why don't we do a double act together? Do you know a little joke?' He said, 'Yes, you!' And that's how it all started – he's been insulting me ever since. He called me his little fat friend who wears a wig. He said, 'You can't see the join,' that I have short fat hairy legs, and I'm mean with money. Now *that* was not true. We never let money come between us. It never got past me! The biggest laugh, of course, was 'Get the tea, Ern.' It never failed.

Do you know, in the forty-three years we were together as partners, we never had an agreement; no written contract; nothing about staying together, sharing the profits, who gets custody of the joke books. I think that says something about togetherness.

As young lads we did everything together – touring, chasing girls, going to the cinema and, of course, performing. When we got married our private lives diverged, but so hectic was our working life that we saw a lot of each other in the

*Eric and Ernie in Blackpool, 1957*

course of any week. We were, I suppose, like brothers who rarely, if ever, quarrelled and could cope with what was an intense partnership without fear of its overheating.

You see, we wanted to do a double act. We started off like Abbott and Costello, straight man and feed, then slowly we became like Laurel and Hardy, two comic characters: the one with the glasses, and the other one with the short fat hairy legs. I can still see him in his raincoat and flat cap, with that bewildered look on his face, giving me a quick hug.

Eric was a very funny man and that's what he was all about: making people laugh.

# Gail Morecambe

The following anecdote by Gail Morecambe, Eric's only daughter, first appeared in print in the book *Hard Act to Follow*, by Michael Sellers and Gary Morecambe. She recalls the time when Gene Pitney was at his zenith, and was invited to appear on a Morecambe and Wise show.

Like many teenage girls of that time, I thought Gene Pitney was rather gorgeous. Knowing this, Dad invited me along to the studios and said I could probably meet Mr Pitney after he'd done his spot on their show. I should have known better.

After Gene Pitney had performed his song, the producer informed him that, due to a technical hitch, he would have to sing it again. Unfortunately for the poor man, he had to sing it five times in all. After the third time, Dad joined him on the set to help him with the delay while the recording was checked. After a few moments of banter with Pitney and the audience – which Dad was brilliant at – Dad suddenly announced, 'My daughter is in love with you.' I think poor Mr Pitney said something like 'Oh, that's nice.' Then Dad said, 'She's in the audience tonight, would you like to meet her? Stand up, Gail. Where are you?'

Many thoughts flashed through my mind at this point, some of them murderous, but I decided it would be better to stand up quickly, smile and sit down again. Rows of heads turned round to see where I was. Mr Pitney kindly said, 'Oh, she's lovely,' to which my father replied, 'Yes, we call her sparrow legs.' I was very self-conscious about my skinny legs and now I wished I'd worn trousers and hoped I wouldn't meet meet Gene Pitney after the show.

■ (Gary: Gail went on to point out that at this time she, being Eric's teenage daughter, was getting much unwanted attention from the press that I, fortunately, wasn't getting. I have to say that until I was about fifteen it all went somewhat over my head. But I do sympathize with how difficult it must have been for Gail. As she says, 'My father knew how I felt, but I don't think he really understood why I felt it. He did try to help matters by not being at home himself if the press asked to interview me. As it was, they wanted only to talk about Dad (understandably) and they would always ask if he was around – sometimes the moment they walked through the front door. If he was in, they'd ask if he could join us for one or two photographs. The few moments of chat with Dad were what they used for the story, and the interview with me would feel like a total waste of time.')

Joan, Gail and Eric, 1970

Steven with Eric and
Ernie, 1979

# Steven Morecambe

Steven is Eric's second son. He has many fond memories of
Eric, the following being one of his favourites.

Iused to have to go and say goodnight to Dad. I'd walk into the
room and he'd be smoking a pipe or cigar and having a glass of
whisky or something. I'd go and kiss him goodnight and he'd pass
me over the whisky. I'd take a sip and then he'd give me a puff of his
cigar or pipe. I'd say, 'Thank you very much,' and start to leave the
room. Just before I got out of the door he'd say, 'Whatever you do,
don't tell your mother, otherwise you'll get me into trouble.'

# David Lightfoot

David Lightfoot, who is a county library manager based in Preston, Lancashire, sent the following brief memory of Eric. In his covering letter, he explained that it is his mother's story.

It was circa 1945, and the venue was Her Majesty's Theatre, Carlisle. Morecambe and Wise were one of the acts in a variety show. Between two of the acts, Morecambe and Wise came on and invited myself and another young girl on to the stage. We were told the orchestra would play various tunes and we had to guess whose signature tune each one was ('Wakey-Wakey' was Billy Cotton's and so on).

They played 'I Do Like to Be Beside the Seaside' and it was my turn to answer. I didn't have a clue. Eric was miming, trying to help me, then he began climbing up the wall at the side of the stage (supposed to be Blackpool Tower) and climbing out of the orchestra pit (the organ appearing from under the stage).

The audience were roaring with laughter, and I was standing there without a clue. I never forgot the name of Reginald Dixon, who played the organ at Blackpool.

Eric gave me a powder compact in a black velvet pouch, which I used for years.

■ (Gary: In his early, formative years, Eric loved all the prat-falling and the visual elements of comedy. At that stage of his career, he was very much in the mould of the clown or the silent movie star, as the above memory testifies.)

Eric and Joan

# Bill Drysdale

Bill Drysdale, who is a psychologist, is an old family friend. He has been a close friend of Gary Morecambe since they were aged four, and spent many happy hours in Eric's company, both at home and on holiday.

At my parents' silver wedding anniversary many years ago, Eric and Joan were among the guests. Eric was constantly hanging around me making comments and interjections.

At that time, there were loads of my parents' friends quizzing me about my career prospects, as I had just started at Oxford University. I mentioned that I was studying French, but was also interested in studying psychology, although I hadn't made any firm decisions yet.

'I see. So you are keeping your options open?' said one guest.

'Yes, it's the way he walks,' interrupted Eric.

☆

One evening, Gary and I were watching the Hitchcock masterpiece *The Birds*. There was one scene featuring an old woman who really did look pretty unpleasant.

'Look! There's the head crow,' said Eric.

Another evening we were watching a popular space adventure series called *UFO*. Eric wanted to watch something else, and Gary said, 'But Dad, it's *UFO*.'

'Tough,' he replied. '*You* F O. I want to watch the other side.'

☆

A photographer once went to Eric's home to do some shots of Eric and Gary for a book. The photographer got closer and closer with his camera. It was quite amusing because the lens ended up only inches away from Eric's nose.

'If you get any closer we'll be in the camera,' said Eric.

☆

When Eric wrote comedy material, he often tried some of it on me and Gary. One I recall: 'Did you hear about Hill William, the Hill Billy who made good?'

☆

Enough of the fun and nonsense: the main point I should get across was that Eric had a real intensity about his comedy that has never really been acknowledged. Often in Morecambe and Wise shows, everyone would be cracking up – but never Eric. In fact, he would be merciless, like a boxer going in for the kill, and his ad-libbing would get even funnier and more outrageous – but he never succumbed to giggles himself. In having this intensity he is like a subsequent generation of comic actors, such as John Cleese and Rowan Atkinson: where he differed, of course, was in his absolute love of show business – for instance, Hollywood musicals – as against the more detached attitude of Cleese and Atkinson. Rowan once told me that BBC Television Centre is just like any other factory, but instead of making tin cans, they make television programmes. I could never imagine Eric thinking like that.

One of my strongest memories of Eric is the constant 'cat and mouse' games that Gary and I used to play with him. We would end up doing things like ducking behind a wall to crawl past, unseen, by the sitting-room window in order to get a football net out without Eric noticing. We knew that if he did he wouldn't be able to resist joining in. When we were slightly older, it became a case of sneaking back from the pub and up to Gary's room without Eric noticing. If he did spot us, he would ask us all into the lounge to watch a video of an old Morecambe and Wise show, no matter how many of us there were. The funny thing is, I didn't really mind either way, but I know it was very frustrating for Gary.

In many ways, I think of Eric as someone who didn't fit into the world of adults. When I was a child, the first thing that struck me about him was that he was around during

the day. Extraordinary! I had always thought of dads as people who went out to work during the day. Then I noticed that there were all sorts of adults' events which Eric went along to, but where he clearly didn't fit in – such as my parents' silver-wedding party at the local golf club, which I mentioned earlier. In that particular case, I thought it was brilliant as it meant both Eric and Joan spent a lot of time with *me* – Eric, of course, spending much of the time subtly taking the mickey out of the other guests.

I remember being surprised by the one time he was serious with Gary and me. We had just made a tape-recording of Gary on guitar and me on the drums. Frankly, it was crap – all the numbers sounded the same – but at the time we thought it OK. Anyway, at the end of the day Gary took the tape home with him, and he must have played it to Eric, because the next thing I knew, Eric was on the phone to me. He kept saying how impressed he was, and I kept waiting for the killer punchline. It never came. He really liked it. It was the most disconcerting moment of my life: Eric never took things seriously – and yet, thinking about it now, I realize that music was very important to him. I think he had a lot of untapped musical talent, rather like Rowan, interestingly. My mother always said Eric was a beautiful mover when he danced, full of rhythm. There again, she always had the hots for Eric!

What was the real Eric Morecambe like? I think there were lots of Eric Morecambes –

funny, intense, cynical, enthusiastic. Occasionally he became preoccupied with serious political issues, such as social unrest on a large scale.

I wonder if he feared he might lose everything. In my clinical work, I have come across a number of rags-to-riches cases, and in each case the patient feared losing all their material possessions, because then they would be back to being nothing. In other words, material wealth equalled everything, because it was the opposite of being poor; and poverty really sucks. If you were poor, you were a nobody – no matter what sort of person you were, or what your skills were, you were nothing.

Understandable, maybe, but also sad. And yet, if that's true about Eric, how come he was never vulgar, tasteless or flashy with his money? I know his wife, Joan, made sure he was careful with money, but even so...

■ (Gary: I recall all Bill has said. I particularly remember – on the social-issue front – Eric telling us that society was crumbling at grass-roots level, and that one day people would take to the streets and that there would be mass rioting. This was in the late sixties, and we had a good chuckle over what we saw as a lot of nonsense. Then came the summer riots of 1981. Unfortunately, my father had a long memory...)

Eric on the steps of his house, 1970

# John Fisher

John Fisher has produced *Parkinson, Des O'Connor Tonight* and
*Heroes of Comedy*. He is also one of the talents to recently bring back
Morecambe and Wise to the commercial channels. He is a great
comedy buff, and author of several books about comedy and
comedians.

I first met Morecambe and Wise in 1973, having admired
them from afar since they began to appear regularly on
*Sunday Night at the London Palladium* in the early sixties.
Remember that routine about the man who sold cigars
opposite the theatre? That dates from then. They were now
due to appear on *Parkinson* and I was assigned to research
their spot. It was around the time that their first volume of
autobiography was to be published by W. H. Allen, and I was
invited to the launch party. Imagine my surprise when the
following day *The Times* reported on the event, with a
photograph of Eric and Ernie standing side by side. Looking
between them is a stray, anonymous face. You've guessed!
Eventually, I got a book signed by the pair. Ernie wrote: 'To
Mr Showbusiness', to which Eric added, 'Yes, but what do
you do for a living?'

To them both I owe that publication of my picture in the
broadsheet press; but sadly, Eric, it made no difference: I'm
still looking for a proper job.

# Ernest Maxin

Ernest Maxin was producer of *The Morecambe and Wise Show* at the BBC from 1975 to 1977, and choreographed their shows from 1970 to 1977. Often the butt of practical jokes played by Eric, he particularly remembers one on location for the 1976 Christmas show.

I always look through the viewfinder on the camera to make sure all the shots are exactly right and to finalize when I'm going to pull back and so on. This is very important and makes a difference to the laughter you're going to get when you see it on the screen. If you pull away too early or too late, you can lose the laugh completely. For instance, Eric was funnier when he was doing certain things in different lengths and, sometimes, he was even funnier from the back. So I was always checking that everything was just right.

One day, while we were on location with John Thaw and Dennis Waterman, I spent a hell of a lot of time looking through the camera. Eventually, we finished and went back to Television Centre.

When it was time to go home, I got on the Tube and sat down, and the guy opposite winked at me. Then I looked across the carriage and there was a woman giggling at me. I thought I'd got into a carriage full of lunatics and didn't feel at all comfortable. The same thing happened in the next carriage.

When finally I reached home, my wife opened the door and gave me a bemused look. What Eric had done was put charcoal and chalk round the viewfinder of the camera. Furthermore, he'd come up to me and said things like 'I like the way you've had your sideboards done,' while tracing his finger round the side of my face and eyes. I remember wondering at the time what the hell he was doing.

What he'd done, of course, was draw a pair of glasses on my face with his finger.

At the climax of the 'Singin' in the Rain' routine, in which Ernie did his Gene Kelly number, Eric had to lie in a horse-trough full of water. And if it didn't work the first time, he knew he'd have to do it again. In the end, we had to shoot it three times because on the first two takes everything went perfectly until Eric got into the trough, when the water splashed too high. I didn't want that: I wanted him to sit sedately in the water.

Now you have to remember this was a time when Eric wasn't too well. With his heart condition, we didn't want to risk his getting pneumonia, so the routine took a long time to complete. This wasn't because of the length of time rehearsing it or the routine itself – Eric did each take perfectly, like a real pro. No, the time was taken up by having to dry him so he didn't catch cold, and then changing his costume.

# Margaret Day

Margaret Day and her husband, Jeff, have been close friends of the Morecambe family for over thirty years. Margaret has many happy memories of Eric.

Although Eric was very clever, bordering on genius, he was, very endearingly, a little boy at heart. When I used to arrive at the Morecambe house with birthday gifts for Joan and Stevie (Eric's second son), being late March it was often near Easter, so I took them Easter eggs, too.

Eric would confront me, carrier bag in hand. 'Is there anything for me in that bag, Mags?'

Joan: 'Eric, you're awful.'

Me, archly: 'There might be.'

Eric: 'Is it dark?'

Me, handing over a large bar of dark chocolate: 'Yes.'

He would then disappear happily upstairs.

Joan: 'He's gone to put it in his cupboard.'

☆

The first time I went to the Morecambe villa in Portugal, I was determined to be the perfect house guest: so when after dinner Eric asked me to play cards with him, I did. I soon sensed something was wrong, for though it was a game of chance, I seemed to be doing all the losing; but I was too polite to say anything. When I went into the kitchen to get him a drink, I said to Joan, 'I think he's cheating.'

Gary said, 'Oh, Dad always cheats.'

☆

Eric and my husband Jeff got on well although they were complete opposites – Eric 'doing the funnies', and Jeff very serious. Eric appeared at our house once having got locked out: he'd forgotten his keys and Joan was out. Eric and Jeff sat

*With Margaret Day*

*The Morecambe family loved Portugal*

watching TV and eating my freshly baked scones. Eric was highly amused when the programme they were watching ended and a cartoon came on, something like *Top Cat* or *Sylvester*. Jeff said, 'We don't want that rubbish,' and switched it off. Eric told me, 'I always watch that programme. I love that cat – he never gives up.'

☆

Eric came round one day and they sat drinking in the sunroom. Eric said, 'I'm going to Morecambe to see George (his father). He's had an operation on his eyes. I'm taking him some books.'

Me, reprovingly: 'Eric!'

Jeff: 'Tell him my carrots are up.'

☆

Sadie (Eric's mother) used to amuse him. Once when she was staying with him I arrived to find him chuckling away. Sadie had looked in the mirror and said, 'My hair's like a pound of candles.' Eric went off chortling, 'A pound of candles!'

When Eric and Ernie were at the height of their careers at the BBC, Joan, Sadie and I were standing in the foyer of Television Centre, waiting to see the show. The studios were newish at the time – lots of glass. Joan asked Sadie what she thought of it. Sadie glanced all around: 'Ee, look at them winders. I'd not like to have to mop this place.' Eric loved that one.

☆

Eric was very good at large problems, but small ones could rattle him. He once rang me saying, 'You were supposed to come for tea today – *don't come.*' He then launched into a chapter of accidents – Mike (his driver) was late, the car wouldn't start, he was ill, Joan was ill, and so on. Before slamming down the phone, he added, 'And Barney [the dog] has been sick on the front doorstep!' Whenever he went on about anything, I'd say, 'And Barney's been sick on the front doorstep,' and make him laugh.

☆

He used to say to Joan and me, 'You two are a better double act than Morecambe and Wise.' He'd give me chapters from a book or a screenplay he was writing and say, 'Ring me tonight and tell me what you think of it.' They were all handwritten and done out of sequence – it just flowed from his pen without his having to rewrite it or make any changes. He used to say that when he retired from showbiz, he would happily just write. I said he did it so effortlessly and so well it made you want to spit.

☆

Jeff and Eric often went together to see Luton Town FC play. Eric would ask little boys there, who had obviously entered the ground without paying, if they would show him how to get in free next week. They always fell for it and said 'Yes' quite seriously.

# Warren Mitchell

The comedian and actor Warren Mitchell became famous through his portrayal of Johnny Speight's bigoted character Alf Garnett. Warren and Eric were firm friends for many years.

I got to know Eric and Joan really well while we were on location in the South of France for *That Riviera Touch*. Eli Wallach was staying at the same hotel as us. He was a big star at the time, and I'd worked with him a short time before.

'Get me to meet him,' urged Eric. 'I'd really like that.'

'Sure, OK,' I said.

One morning, I was sitting with Eric in the lobby when Wallach came striding through. I got up, extended a hand and said, 'Hiya, Eli,' in a matey way.

Wallach gave me a cursory glance without faltering in his step, said a curt 'Good morning' and strode on out of the hotel.

Eric fell about laughing and, from that moment on, whenever and wherever he saw me, he'd call out, 'Hiya, Eli!'

# Michael Aspel

Presenter Michael Aspel – more commonly recognized these days as the man with the 'big red book' – was a longstanding friend of Eric. He first worked with Morecambe and Wise in the late 1960s.

Not many people know about the series of 'trailers' that Eric and Ernie devised with their producer, John Ammonds, and involving myself. The reason not many people know is that the BBC never used them.

For one of these trailers we found a mansion, complete with swimming-pool. Eric and Ernie and I sat under an umbrella, sipping champagne and chatting.

I asked, 'How long have you been together?' Eric said, 'I've been together all my life.' And so on. Eventually Eric asked me if I'd like another drink. I said, 'Yes please,' so he snapped his fingers, and John Ammonds, dressed as a flunkey, dipped a ladle in the swimming-pool and topped up my glass. Pity the BBC never used it. It made me laugh, anyway, as Eric would say.

☆

There was a great moment when we were rehearsing their show in about 1968. I was their 'special guest', and the scene involved

Eric and Ernie with Michael Aspel

me as a desperate man wanting to fling myself off the top of a skyscraper. The boys agree to jump with me out of sympathy. We all rush to the edge, they stop, I go over and they carry on with their lines.

For the show, there were mattresses for me to land on. For the rehearsals, I was supposed to skid to a halt before the edge. But I got over-enthusiastic, sailed on and landed with a crash among the lights and bits of equipment several feet below. I lay there blinking, and Eric's face slowly appeared over the top, grinning wickedly. I can't remember what he said, but when I laughed it hurt.

That was the first show in which he did his famous exit at the end, with cap, raincoat and carrier bag.

Thames Television stars, with their wives

# Bill Franklyn

Actor Bill Franklyn's appearances in the long-running Schweppes ('Schhhh, you know who') TV ads are still well remembered. His work with Eric and Ernie included the film *The Intelligence Men* and a Morecambe and Wise television show.

In the early fifties, my father, Leo Franklyn, was playing Dame in panto at the Golders Green Hippodrome, and I went to a matinée. Before I went to my seat Dad said, 'The robbers are off this afternoon, and another younger double act who've been playing small parts are on for the two robbers. Tell me what you think of them.'

Dad and I were, for once in our lives, prophets. Afterwards, in Dad's dressing-room: 'Not since Sid Field and Groucho have I laughed so much. Dad, they're very special, and...'

Dad added, 'I thought you'd like them. I sniffed it at the rehearsal this morning, when we knew they'd have to go on, that they were a bit tasty.'

Eric and Ernie were, for Dad and me, launched.

☆

One abiding memory is from the making of the Morecambe and Wise film *The Intelligence Men*. Sitting in a semicircle on the set, waiting for the lighting as ever, were, in this order, Eric, Bill (Franklyn), Francis Matthews, Ernie, Terry Alexander and Richard Vernon. And standing very adjacent to centre was Warren Mitchell.

Eric gave us a fifteen-minute introduction to the secrets of comedy and how it should be played. The quick-cut close-ups of the listeners and the mutual reactions have remained for ever in my cutting-room head.

Enjoying someone's company and looking forward to the next day's work with them – that summarizes my time with Eric.

Eric (without a second's hesitation): Mr Do-do.

Collapse of me, the director and the entire crew. So we kept it in.

Later in the scene, when Eric's character was told he had to go to another office, he said, 'Certainly,' then added, 'Oh, and can Mr Do-do come?' Eric was not going to let a gag go to waste, and for the rest of the film, when ever I appeared, he said, 'Hello, Mr Do-do.'

☆

When I was filming episodes of *Paul Temple* for the BBC, and Eric and Ernie were recording their classic shows, we often had next-door dressing-rooms. Once, after coffee and chats in my room, Eric was called back on set. He got up, said 'See you later, Fran,' left and locked me in my room. It was fifteen minutes before our floor-manager came to let me out.

Again, while I was filming with Eric at Pinewood, my wife, Angela, was working on another set and Eric kept asking when he was going to meet her. One day (by now Eric was well aware that her name was Angela) she joined us for lunch. When she arrived, he grabbed her hand and said, with a big wink at me, 'So this is that Elizabeth you keep telling me about!' Then, in a loud stage whisper, 'Don't worry, your secret is safe with me.'

☆

There are so many more hysterical times with him that I could be boring, but there was the other, secret, Eric that few of the public or his colleagues were allowed to see. His painting and writing; his escape to the countryside to fish and bird-watch, and be silent. It was this other side of the clown that could be contemplative and tender.

After we had all attended the Manchester première of *The Intelligence Men*, and the public frenzy had died down, he, myself and Angela found ourselves together, out on the deserted pavements, and hungry. Eric guided us to a basement club he knew, the only place that would serve so late.

Angela was then very pregnant with our second son and feeling very vulnerable. In the midst of this wonderful quiet time together, Eric grabbed her hand, asked her to dance, and waltzed her romantically around the floor. She told me later that he'd said he thought a pregnant woman was the most beautiful thing in the world. It was an instinctive and genuine compliment from a very sensitive man and left her up in the air with joy.

How we miss him.

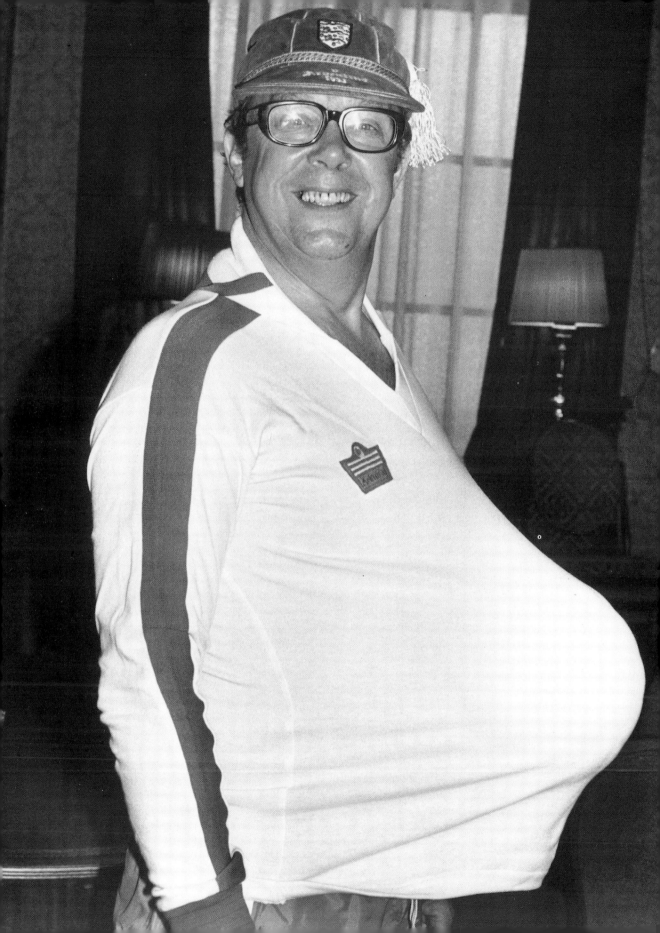

# Muriel Young

Former television presenter Muriel Young has been a friend of the
Morecambe family since the mid-sixties.

All my memories of Eric are so happy – all the laughs we had... so many...
we never stopped – though we all saw each other more in Portugal than
at home, as we were all up to our eyes in work.

I think my most lasting memory of Eric is from the very early days of our
visits to the Algarve, around 1963-64, when everything was orchards right
down to the sea – no blocks of flats – and earnest young boys, not more than
eleven or twelve, were the only available caddies at the recently completed
Vila Maura Golf Club, which had been carved out of a pine forest.

Cyril (Muriel's late husband, the producer Cyril Coke) and Eric were no
great golfers, but loved it. Eric got very upset that day, because no end of
larking about could raise a grin on the serious little faces of the two 'caddies'
– of course, they didn't understand English and had no idea of Eric's
standing.

Finally it got Eric down – he just couldn't raise a titter. However, when a
ball went into the rough under some pine trees, he disappeared from view,
returning a moment later with a pine cone stuck up either side of his jumper.
He had better boobs than Samantha Fox! The two young boys broke down,
rolled around on the ground and screamed with laughter – and they didn't
stop all the way round the course. It was probably the best laugh of their
lives. I might add that Cyril wasn't much better.

What lovely days they were.

# Sid Green

Sid Green, together with the late Dick Hills, was Eric and Ernie's scriptwriter during their early successful television outings (1961–67) for Lew Grade's ATV.

Morecambe and Wise were different from any other double act because it was almost as though they couldn't care less about you, me or the audience: they were just doing it for themselves.

Eric had a very strong personality and when he was on he was always in charge. Television is just about faces and Eric's face was made for television. He looked so innocent. You could get away with the most outrageous innuendoes when writing for Eric, because nobody believed he was being rude with that face.

# Ann Hamilton

Actress and regular straight woman for Eric and Ernie throughout their BBC years, Ann Hamilton got to know Eric in his working environment arguably better than anyone except Ernie.

I remember arriving at rehearsal one day wearing a midi – fashion of the day – full-length coat made up in a tapestry fabric. Eric took one look and said, 'She's wearing the sofa!' I took off the coat to reveal crushed-velvet trousers and bolero, and he added, 'And the curtains.'

After Eric's first illness, when daily rehearsals were shortened into one session with a very quick lunch break, Eric used to bring in an apple and a piece of cheese. I suggested making some soup and taking that in. Eric accepted with alacrity, insisting on his favourite 'Pea and ham, which must be thick enough to trot a donkey across.' From then on, pea and ham soup was order of the day, with Eric frequently asking for 'another slice'.

Studio days could become a little hectic and occasionally tempers a smidge frayed. In the show where Shirley Bassey was to

*Eric in 'The Intelligence Men'*

Eric with Ann Hamilton

# Gordon Beningfield

The artist and naturalist Gordon Beningfield, who died in May 1998, was possibly Eric's closest friend. They spent many a day on the riverbank together.

have a number 'improved' by Eric and Ernie, the lady from Tiger Bay didn't look too happy when she appeared on the set in a shimmering silver dress, until Eric said, 'You look just like a Brillo pad.' Shirley burst out laughing, the atmosphere was broken and her rendering of 'Smoke Gets in Your Eyes' leading to her exit in outsize workman's boots was truly hilarious.

☆

On one of his fishing trips Eric popped into the theatre at Swindon, where my husband was director and we had a flat over the theatre. During tea my husband said to Eric, 'When are you going to come and do a show here?' Eric asked how many seats there were, and on being told 617 retorted, 'Big enough for me – not big enough for Ernie.'

The BBC was filming a documentary which I was to appear in. I was on the river holding a fishing rod and trying to look fairly professional for the cameras. In truth, I was having a lot of difficulty catching any fish. It reached the point of desperation when the producer suggested someone should run down to the nearest village and buy a fish to stick on the end of my line.

I was standing around growing more and more frustrated by my lack of success, when at that moment a tweed-clad figure appeared in the distance. I recognized this as being my friend Eric Morecambe.

He had come to do a spot of fishing by himself, and, without showing me any recognition, he sat down on the opposite bank and prepared to start fishing. The last person the BBC would have expected to turn up on a peaceful Hertfordshire riverbank was Eric. And I had no intention of telling them. Then they asked me who it was who had sat down to fish across the river. 'Oh, just another fisherman who comes down here from time to time,' I said.

He was temporarily forgotten as we concentrated on me trying to catch a fish. Meanwhile, in contrast to my lack of success, Eric was reeling in fish after fish, and it hadn't gone unnoticed by my company. I was beginning to feel slightly uneasy about all this.

Typical of Eric, he could not resist finally crossing the water and heading towards us. With a smile he said, 'Hello Gordon, how are you getting on?'

It was wonderful, for as soon as he spoke there was a split second of complete silence followed by a unison 'Good God, it's Eric Morecambe.' It was quite some bonus for them.

A few days later, I watched a run-through of the programme, and as it reached the end I could be seen talking to Eric, whose back was towards the cameras. And at the very end, he slowly turned round, removed his glasses and chuckled in his easy, recognizable manner. That was all he needed to do for everyone watching the programme to know who he was.

■ (Gary: I think Eric saw in Gordon someone with whom he could just be himself. Or, as Gordon put it, someone with whom he could behave and do exactly as he wanted – 'and believe me, he did.')

# Bette Hill

Bette Hill, widow of motor-racing legend Graham Hill, and mother of the 1996 Formula One world champion, Damon Hill, like all the members of her family has had a long, long friendship with the Morecambe family.

The thing that I remember about Eric (one of them!) was at Graham's forty-fifth birthday party at Lyndhurst, Shenley. My mother-in-law, Connie, a great character and loved by all of our friends, got into a giggling act with Eric. He was being particularly gracious to her, and she was lapping it up. She became hysterical when he put his very long Cuban cigar under her nose and did a Groucho Marx impression. We all fell about, and she absolutely loved it.

■ (Gary: Eric's adoration of Groucho was equalled only by his adoration of Phil Silvers. Not only did Eric often impersonate – and very finely, too – Groucho Marx, but the skip-dance that Eric and Ernie did at the end of each of their shows was a lift from Groucho doing a similar one in an early Marx Brothers movie.)

Eric as Groucho, Ernie as Lana Turner!

# Mike Yarwood

The impressionist Mike Yarwood was at his zenith at the BBC at the same time Eric and Ernie were at theirs.

I never actually worked with them, of course, but we were always there together. In fact, for a while John Ammonds was producing *The Morecambe and Wise Show* and my show simultaneously. He would finish with Eric and Ernie, then come and tell me how good their show was. Eric told me that he did exactly the same with them.

I was arriving at the Beeb once, when Eric, getting out of a taxi with Ernie and Glenda Jackson, shouted, 'Harold!' Everyone knew I was doing Harold Wilson at the time. I made the fatal mistake of turning round and reacting. I went up to Eric and told him that I was doing an impression of him nowadays. 'Really?' said Eric. 'Are you doing me now?' You had to be there. So quick on his feet.

☆

On one occasion, we were at Downing Street together. Eric whispered to me, 'Have you seen that woman over there? She looks like a fish.' He was right: she did look like a fish. Eventually, she came over to where we were standing. She said to Eric, 'You don't remember me.'

Yes,' said Eric, 'I saw you on the cold slab at Macfisheries!'

I was doubled up with laughter. A wonderfully, naturally funny man.

# Bobby Caplin

Bobby Caplin was working at the Batley Variety Club at the time of Eric's first heart attack in 1968.

Many people only saw Eric on television, but for the greater part of the year he'd be touring. There were summer seasons at Blackpool or Great Yarmouth, pantomime and clubs such as Batley. He spent a tremendous amount of time travelling, being on his own.

The night he had his first heart attack, he'd been appearing at Batley with Ernie. I'd arranged to have dinner with him after the show. About half an hour before going on stage, he came to me and he was looking a bit ill. He said he didn't feel good and had a pain in his arm.

'Do you mind if we don't have dinner tonight?' he asked. 'I just want to get back to the hotel straight after the show.'

'Not at all,' I said.

It's a good job he did, because he'd just got into Leeds when he had his terrible heart attack.

# Dave Allen

Comedian Dave Allen never worked with Eric and Ernie, but he was at the height of his BBC career at the same time as Morecambe and Wise were.

Eric made you smile: if you talk to people about Eric Morecambe – and I don't mean only people who knew him personally – they always smile.

Eric made it all look very easy and spontaneous. But that was the result of all those years of tough slog and the number-two dates in variety, the result of being rejected and the bad crits. That kind of experience comes to the fore when things start going right for you and you have the ability to take charge. And Eric had that ability in abundance.

It was typical of Eric to turn his health problems into a comedy routine. I remember him telling me about his first heart attack in 1968. He'd had the attack in the car and couldn't drive. He'd managed to get the window down and sat there hoping a passer-by would come past before he died. His description of what happened when

Walter Butterworth came along and got him to the hospital was wonderful. Yet even as I was laughing at him telling me this, I remember thinking, 'The man nearly died and he's being so funny about it.' But Eric had the ability, you see, even in the middle of all that trauma, to be aware that there was some great comedy in it and to register it for the future.

In this age of supposed political correctness, many comedians would be worried about implying a woman had a beautiful pair of breasts. Not Eric. He loved innuendo and *double-entendres* about buttocks or breasts or legs. But he never downgraded anyone with innuendo: he had a wonderful ability to convey the message clearly without saying the actual words. And the audience always went with the implication.

# Mike Fountain

For many years, right up to the time of Eric's sudden death, Mike Fountain was his chauffeur and general factotum.

When I was driving him home from a TV show, Eric would insist on getting some reaction on how it had gone. He would gather opinions from Joan and the kids, if they were in the car, and from me. He'd spend the first three-quarters of the journey home questioning us. He was really worried about every show after he'd done it. He just had to get a reaction from as many different people as possible about how it had gone.

Eric had a curious attitude to money. Say he wanted to go into town to get some tobacco. He'd say to Joan, 'Can you give me some money?'

'How much do you want?' she'd ask.

'Give me twenty.'

'Twenty! What do you want twenty for?'

'It doesn't matter. Just give me twenty.'

'All right.'

Now, he probably only needed a fiver for what he wanted, but then he'd come back to the house and hide the rest. Later on, when he wanted something really big, he'd have maybe a hundred and fifty to two hundred quid stashed away upstairs, which he could use without asking Joan for more money. That was a really funny trait of his.

# Kenneth Tynan

The author and critic Kenneth Tynan was one of the leading cultural figures of the radical 1960s, as well as deviser of the notorious nude revue *Oh Calcutta!* He spent some time with Eric during 1973 to write a profile of him for the *Observer Magazine*. The resulting article was one of the most perceptive and positive personal appraisals Eric ever received.

Specifically looking for signs of melancholy in Eric, Tynan admitted he could discern none. Instead, he perceived Eric to be the possessor of 'the most devastatingly incisive brain in comedy', and noted how he could shift through a whole series of comic moods like alarm, aggression, collapse, recovery and snide insinuation all in about four seconds. 'Morecambe's reflexes,' he wrote, 'the effortless speed and timing with which he changes expressions and tones of voice, are among the wonders of the profession. He has burgeoned into one of the most richly quirkish and hypnotic performers on the box.'

Calling *The Morecambe and Wise Show* 'brilliant, wholly original and irresistible', Tynan wrote, 'How much of it is due to Eddie Braben's scripts and how much to the performers is hard to determine: but we know that the scripts are heavily modified in rehearsal and that most of the changes come from Eric.'

Tynan's admiration for Eric was such that it was he who urged Laurence Olivier to accept an invitation to make a brief appearance on the 1973 *Morecambe and Wise Christmas Show.*

# Eddie Braben

Eddie Braben became writer of *The Morecambe and Wise Show* in 1968, taking over from Sid Green and Dick Hills.

The impression I always got was that Eric knew he was being stupid on stage. You'd see the glint and then it was a case of 'Look at me – look what I'm going to do now.'

When Eric and Ernie joined the BBC, Bill Cotton rang me at home and asked, 'How would you like to write for Morecambe and Wise?'

At first I said no: I really did, because I didn't think it would work. But Bill said to come down and meet the boys, anyway. It was always 'the boys'. They were in their forties then, and if they were together now it would still be 'the boys'.

When I first met them, I watched mannerisms and the attitude between them. I could see there was real affection between Eric and Ernie. It was more than affection. They were like two brothers. In fact, they were closer than any brothers I've ever seen. And I thought, if I could get that affection across to an audience, I would be halfway home. That's what I wanted, and what I like to think I captured.

Writing the Christmas show was the worst. It was a killer. People were judging the quality of their Christmas by *The Morecambe and Wise Show*. If they didn't like the show, they had a bad Christmas. That was an awful thing to have hanging over you. Of course, it was gratifying to have audiences of 28.5 million, but the pressure was enormous.

I've no doubt that health suffers as a result of all these pressures – as I know myself. Eric's health certainly suffered because he gave so much. He would never relax when he was working. I've worked with a lot of big names, but I've never seen anyone give as much as he did. He gave everything. Well, in the end, he *did* give everything. He couldn't have given any more.

In many ways, Eric was his own worst enemy, because he never, ever, stopped doing the jokes. He always had to give a performance: he didn't stop with me, even when we were on our own. In fact, I said to him once, 'For Christ's sake, Eric, back off. I've heard them all. And three of them you've just done, *I* wrote.'

# Glenda Jackson

Formerly an international star of stage and screen, and now an MP,
Glenda Jackson is regarded as the actress who made it right to be seen
on a Morecambe and Wise show.

The first time I met Eric was in one of those tiny hospitality rooms which the
BBC still had then at Shepherd's Bush. And I ached with laughter at listening
to his stories and anecdotes about variety.

I'll always remember his practical note of advice to me when we were
rehearsing my first Morecambe and Wise show. He just said, 'Louder and faster.'

I also remember seeing Eric and Ernie do a sketch in their BBC series where
they did nothing but sit on a bench, and I was rolling about on the floor with
laughter.

When I met them later, I told them how much I'd enjoyed that sketch, and Eric
turned to me and said, 'But it was awful. The studio audience didn't laugh once.'

I found that extraordinary, because it had been a brilliant piece of TV humour.
But Eric did have the belief that you only know you've got it right if the audience
laughs. If the audience doesn't laugh, you've failed.

The great thing about Eric was that he never begged. Some comedians come
on and almost say, 'Love me, love me.' Eric never did, because he respected his
audience.

I was offered the leading role in *A Touch of Class* as a direct result of working
with Eric and Ernie: the producer of the film saw me on *The Morecambe and Wise
Show*.

When I won my second Oscar for the film, I received a telegram from Eric
which read: 'Stick with us, kid, and we'll get you a third!'

I don't think there was anybody in the whole of the British theatre who
wouldn't have given their back teeth to work with Eric Morecambe.

# Doug McKenzie

Photographer Doug McKenzie took many shots of Eric and Ernie, notably at Royal Shows.

We were flying back from a show in Jersey. I was seated next to Ernie, and Eric was seated next to my assistant, Ann-Marie. He'd been constantly making everyone on the plane laugh. Eric's wife, Joan, was seated in front of them. Eric kept telling Ann-Marie, in a loud voice, that once Joan was asleep they'd 'be all right'. After a while, he suddenly pounced on Ann-Marie and shouted, 'She's asleep!'

# André Previn

The conductor André Previn joined Morecambe and Wise in what is, arguably, their most celebrated television routine, when Eric played Grieg – and lost. In 1974, three years after that famous appearance, Previn wrote,

'The boys have always been extremely kind and courteous to me: Eric never fails to apologize both before and after he hits me. I have been given to understand that they will ask me back to work with them again – as soon as they can think of further humiliation to put me through. What's more, I look forward to it a great deal.'

# Dickie Davies

The Morecambe family first met sports-presenter Dickie Davies while on holiday in Portugal, which is the setting for his first story.

We all met up in Portugal one year. There were quite a few of us, as both families had brought friends with them. We went to a restaurant in Albufeira one evening, and as we left we decided it would be nice to have an ice-cream.

Joan organized the purchasing and passing out of these ice-creams and we all sat down at a terraced cafe to eat them. Despite the twelve or more ice-creams she'd bought, she had somehow managed to overlook Eric. He kept mumbling on all the time we ate ours, almost making us feel guilty.

'Marvellous,' he said, with a look of sadness on his face. 'I bring everyone out here on holiday, I'm the head of the family, and I'm the one who gets forgotten.'

The ice-creams were inside paper cups, and as the first of us finished I remember him picking up the cup and doing his full Schnozzle Durante bit – 'Sittin' at my piano the other day'.

What truly impressed me was that suddenly he was an international comedian, because of this visual act he was putting over. The local people were hysterical as they thronged around him doing this ad-lib performance.

☆

Just prior to his heart bypass operation in 1979, Eric had been quite ill and he decided he needed somewhere he could get away and hide. So he came to stay with us, and although we were delighted to have him it was also a responsibility.

The bypass operation was still in its infancy then, and he was very worried about it. He never wanted to go to bed or to be on his own. There were times when we would drink and talk until three or four in the morning. On the Friday night, I was preparing for *World of Sport* the next day and I had to be in the studio at 8.00 a.m. I looked at the clock and it was 3.00 a.m.

I said, 'Eric, I've got to go. I've got a four-and-a-half-hour programme tomorrow. I've got to get to bed.'

'Oh,' he said glumly. 'So it's me and the valium, is it?'

His health was better after his operation, but he clearly wasn't right. I asked him, 'Why are you continuing to work? You've just written a very successful novel and you obviously love writing. Why don't you concentrate on that?'

'I'm not sure I have enough,' he replied.

'Enough *money*?' I said. 'You've got a

*Eric and his prized Rolls Royce cars*

Rolls-Royce; you've got a chauffeur; and you've got a lovely home. More importantly, you have a beautiful wife and the family are all around you. What more do you need?'

'Yeah,' he said. 'But when you get older, you need a bit of money.'

Now that was a funny thing to come from Eric, because he was an extremely kind and generous man – he wasn't miserly at all. But that was his background talking.

■ (Gary: Eric and Dickie worked together once, when Eric appeared on the Christmas edition of *World of Sport*. The idea was that Eric was supposed to be attending a *World of Sport* Christmas party, but had arrived early – right at the start of the show instead of the end. It proved a good way to get him on the programme and, as Dickie said, 'Eric totally ad-libbed for the whole two and a half hours. I discovered that if you do work with E. Morecambe Esquire, he won't let you come out of it badly, as long as you contribute to the humour as a straight man, and don't try to be the big personality yourself.')

# Mickey Lunn

Mickey Lunn was ghillie on the stretch of the River Test where Eric loved to fish.

I first met Eric with Dickie Davies. Dickie left us and Eric and I went off to the river together. He was edgy and I knew this was a man who was living on his nerves. He suddenly produced a paper bag – God alone knows where he got it from – and started doing his paper-bag trick, throwing up an imaginary pebble and pretending to catch it. And he kept on doing this.

I wondered if I was ever going to get this guy relaxed. I practically had to grab him by the throat and push him up against a tree.

'Are you going to go fishing or not?' I demanded.

He gave me a look at what he could do by casting a fly. He did it quite reasonably and I thought that, yes, I could get him to relax and catch a fish. Sure enough, he did relax and it did him the power of good.

# Penelope Keith

The actress Penelope Keith has been a household name since she appeared in the sit-coms *The Good Life* and *To the Manor Born*. She struck up a good friendship with Eric following her appearance in the 1977 *Morecambe and Wise Christmas Show*.

I first met Eric in the 1960s at ATV, when I was working there for a while. And I found it extraordinary the way how, when Eric walked into a room, everyone looked round and smiled. Now, we weren't demanding that he be funny but, because we all smiled, he obviously felt the need to respond through this amazing comic gift he had. And it must have been awful for him, because he must have been thinking, 'Oh hell, they want me to be funny.'

But he did it. And he was always so kind and courteous to all the people he encountered in the Morecambe and Wise shows.

A sketch in the 1977 Christmas show in which I appeared required a group of army gymnasts, and when they arrived to rehearse, Eric made a point of going over to them to say hello and to have a joke.

Eric always seemed to be the driving force in that partnership. He was the one who was working, working, working. I'm not suggesting Ernie Wise wasn't working hard – of course he was. But it always seemed to be Eric who was controlling it, particularly on the creative side.

# Rowan Atkinson

Although the comedian Rowan Atkinson never worked with Eric, he had a chance to study him at close quarters when he accompanied a mutual friend of Gary Morecambe's to the Morecambe home in 1977. At the time, Atkinson had just embarked on a career in comedy, but was largely unknown beyond the Oxford fringe.

The first thing that struck me about Eric was how funny he was in the house. To me, that was completely alien, because I'm from a totally different comedy culture: one which was more middle-class, less music-hall tradition and more carefully constructed, scripted television tradition.

The people I worked with then – and have continued to work with since – were lawyers and barristers: highly educated people. They were relatively fun-loving but serious-minded people, who weren't cracking jokes all the time. But here was Eric, who blatantly was. And it was extremely impressive to see how natural it was with him.

It was also daunting, because I knew I was nowhere near as funny as that in real life, and I wondered if you really had to be as funny as that around the house in order to have a successful career in comedy. When you meet someone oozing such comic confidence from every pore, it doesn't fill you with confidence yourself. I remember thinking, 'God, how oppressive to be expected to be this funny all the time.' My other thought was to wonder what it must be like for the family to live with this man. My family have never had the concern that I'm going to be relentlessly funny around the house, because I'm exactly the opposite. But Eric's family had to live with this 'act' all the time.

I then started thinking about how difficult Eric must have found it to live with himself. I thought that if he had this natural ability and a need to be funny all the time, what must it be like when he didn't want to be funny, and the pressure remained on him to be so?

# Alan Bennett

Alan Bennett is a playwright and author of international renown. The following anecdote appeared in a broadsheet in 1997, and in Bennett's book *Writing Home*, published that year.

I heard a great story about Eric Morecambe when he and Ernie were making their shows at the BBC. There was a one-armed commissionaire employed there, who was infamous for disliking everybody – except Morecambe and Wise. One day, pausing to chat to Eric as he entered the studios, the commissionaire plucked up the courage to ask him if it would be at all possible for him and his wife to get tickets to watch them record one of the Morecambe and Wise shows.

Eric shook his head and said, 'Oh no, I can't do that.'

'Oh,' said the disappointed commissionaire. 'Why not?'

'You can't clap.'

■ (Gary: This is one of Martin and my all-time Eric favourites, as I remember the commissionaire very well – and how much he laughed afterwards. Actor Phillip Schofield tells this story, too, and adds, 'Needless to say, the gentleman and his wife did get the very best seats for the show.')

# Hannah Gordon

Hannah Gordon has been a popular TV and stage actress for three decades and her 1970s sit-com *My Wife Next Door* is still remembered fondly. She appeared on *The Morecambe and Wise Show* twice in 1973 and again in 1980.

I think it was on a *Morecambe and Wise Christmas Show*. We were standing in front of the tabs with the usual cross-talk going on: Ernie doing the grovelling and Eric being off-hand and uninterested while creating background havoc.

I was wearing a rather baggy-sleeved dress decorated with lace. The sleeves tied at the wrists, and the whole outfit was very presentable.

There was one moment when Eric was insulting me so much that I was supposed to look at my watch and say, 'Well, if I go now I will just be in time to catch my bus.'

Normally I always wear my watch, but because of the design of my dress I'd taken it off in the dressing-room so as to make it possible to tie the sleeves.

When I realized it wasn't there, I decided I must, as a true professional, cover up my bare wrist with my other hand in a natural manner so that no one would notice anything.

Needless to say, Eric caught me out, and right in the middle of filming the spot he turned to me and said, 'You haven't got your watch on, have you?' Then he spun round to the audience and said, 'She hasn't got a her watch on, ladies and gentlemen. What an actress!'

When you are on the legitimate side of the business you are always terribly proud to have covered up an error or whatever. The rules in comedy, I learnt, seemingly differ.

# Alec Guinness

Alec Guinness has become an icon of film and stage – and a cult figure through his appearances in the *Star Wars* trilogy.

I was a great admirer of Eric's, and I still like to see him on the box when there are repeats. I only met him once – when I appeared on *The Morecambe and Wise Show* – and he was delightful.

■ (Gary: Alec Guinness in fact appeared twice with Eric and Ernie, once for the BBC and once for Thames. Perhaps working with them made him feel that once was enough, and he's chosen to erase the memory of the second occasion!

I will always remember that first routine with Guinness, when he appears at Eric's side. Eric gently turns to Ernie and says, 'Look out, there's a drunk come on.')

# Max Bygraves

The entertainer Max Bygraves was one of Eric's peers. They knew each other for years, and Max appeared on a Morecambe and Wise show for Thames Television shortly before Eric died.

What a jester! One lunchtime at Thames Television Studios, we were having a drink at the bar. Eric was telling me about the pacemaker he'd had fitted that week. I was keen to know how a pacemaker functioned. Wide-eyed, Eric explained in detail.
'Do they never go wrong?' I asked.
'Went wrong this morning,' he said.
'What happened?'
'I farted, and the garage door opened.'

# Brian Rix

In response to the authors' request for a memory of Eric, Lord Rix wrote, 'This presents me and my wife, Elspet, with an insurmountable problem. We haven't got one!' But he, too, remembers Eric with affection.

We met Eric (and Joan, of course) at so many charity functions – the Lord's Taverners, the SOS – and he was always immensely entertaining company; generous with his time – to a fault (like another old friend, Leslie Crowther, and many others in the world of show business).

As a family, along with most others in Britain, we watched Eric and Ernie in their Christmas Show every year with devoted appreciation, and we all felt we had lost a personal friend with the sad news of his untimely death.

Like other legends, Eric has many stories told about him, all amusing – even if not always strictly accurate!

# Madeline Bell

Blues singer Madeline Bell met, and worked with, Eric on several occasions. She recalls the time she appeared in a Morecambe and Wise Royal Show.

It was the mid-1970s. We were at the Theatre Royal, Windsor, for a Royal Command Performance in front of HRH Prince Charles.

Eric, who was organizing the artistes backstage, was coming to the end of the pre-show chat when I asked him (I was doing my first Royal Show) how I should address HRH.

Without losing a beat, Eric replied, 'I'm on a first-name basis. I call him "Prince".'

■ (Gary: I was working with Billy Marsh at the time, and Billy's company, London Management, represented Madeline. Knowing I had a modicum of influence over my father – well, as much as any son over his dad – and being a great fan of Madeline's, I asked him if he would consider including her in the forthcoming Royal Show. He didn't find a problem with this, but was more impressed when he heard, via Billy Marsh, that Prince Charles had made the same request.)

# Ronnie Barker

The comic actor Ronnie Barker had a remarkable career before choosing to take early retirement. His television work was extensive and included such delights as *Porridge* and *Open All Hours*; but it is perhaps for his long partnership with Ronnie Corbett in *The Two Ronnies* that he is most fondly remembered.

Eric loved appearing to put people down, to make them look small – but only as a joke, I hasten to add. He was very good at it: very funny. I thought him brilliant; I was an abject fan, and felt very lucky to have been fortunate enough to know him.

He only came to dinner with us once at my house. Richard Beckinsale was invited too, and at eight o'clock we stood, with our wives, waiting for Eric and Joan to appear.

At two minutes past, the doorbell rang, and I opened the door. There stood Eric and Joan, and behind them their chauffeur, waiting for instructions as to when he should return.

Eric poked his head inside the hallway, looked around at the place we are proud to call 'home', noted the guests, and turned to his chauffeur.

'Give it about an hour,' he said.

■ (Gary: Eric and Ronnie must have had a mutual appreciation society going, because Eric often told me how wonderful he thought Ronnie was, as both man and comedian. They corresponded – very amusingly – for a number of years but, as Ronnie implies, didn't see as much of each other as they would have liked.

I was fortunate enough to attend a charity bash where they were seated near each other. Listening to one polished comedian in full flow is enjoyable enough – but two...!)

# Eddie Waters

Eddie Waters, a former picture editor on the *Sun*, has known the Morecambe family for twenty-five years. He acted as Eric's literary agent during the years leading up to Eric's death. Just in passing, Eddie's uncle was Jack Warner – famed as Dixon in *Dixon of Dock Green* – and two of Eddie's aunts were wartime radio stars, the double act Elsie and Doris Waters.

In addition to his great love of pipes, Eric also had a collection of clocks and watches. In the early days of digital wristwatches in the mid-seventies, I came across one that not only told the time, the day and the date, but also made an improper suggestion: 'Lets F***'.

I showed it to Eric, who immediately asked me to buy another one – then another and another, and so on. I think I bought him five or six. I was beginning to think he had a stall in Petticoat Lane. Heaven knows to whom they were being sent!

(Gary: While I was working on this book, Eddie recalled a nerve-racking moment from the time when I appeared on Russell Harty with Eric. Eric was promoting *The Reluctant Vampire*, and I was promoting my book about him, *Funny Man*. It's frightening enough appearing on live prime-time TV with your dad, but it's even worse when, just as you step forward, following the introduction to a live audience and a TV audience of 13 million, your father turns to you and says – in an oblique reference to 'Bring Me Sunshine' – 'Now, you know the words to the song, don't you?')

looking out of the large window, he said, 'What do you think of the garden, Mike? The gardener went out to cut the grass last Thursday and we haven't seen him since.'

☆

I last met Eric Morecambe, face to face, outside the Royal Parish Church of St Martin-in-the-Fields, in Trafalgar Square, on Thursday, 24 March 1983. He was then, as he used to put it, 'half a star'. The occasion was an unforgettable memorial service for the life and work of Arthur Askey. Eric was signing autographs. I joined the back of the queue, holding my head down so that he wouldn't recognize me and anticipate the gag I wanted to pull on him. When the last autograph-hunter had said goodbye, I approached him quickly, and offered him my open chequebook and a pen with the words 'Can you make this out to the Des O'Connor Fan Club?' He went through with the gag, signing the cheque and laughing his wonderful laugh.

I remember saying to him, 'Wasn't Dickie good?' – this being a reference to Dickie Henderson who, as one of Arthur's best friends, had delivered a fantastic address from the pulpit and made that packed congregation roar with laughter with memories and stories of big-hearted Arthur.

I will never forget Eric's reply: 'He was brilliant. In fact, Mike, I'm going to write to him and book him to do mine.'

This was a typical Eric Morecambe line. I didn't take the remark seriously at all; it was just Eric being Eric. It was only at his own funeral that I realized I had misjudged him. Dickie Henderson gave an address.

Shortly afterwards, the BBC asked me to make a tribute programme to Eric for radio. One of the first people I rang to ask to contribute to the programme was Dickie. He was appearing in summer season at Eastbourne. He met me at the station, and during the short car journey to the house I said to him, 'Isn't it funny, when I last spoke to Eric, he said he was so impressed with your address at Arthur's service that he was going to write to you and book you to speak at his – and you did.'

Dickie's answer floored me. 'He *did* write and book me. Do you want to see the letter?'

Later, he showed it to me. I can remember every word of it. Eric typed all his letters with one finger of each hand on his well-worn portable typewriter, which often produced one letter slightly higher than the others and always seemed to need a new ribbon. (You could imagine him writing to Lord Grade on that typewriter: 'Dear Lew, You can see how poor I am by the fact I can't afford a new ribbon for this typewriter...')

His letter to Dickie, written a couple of days after Arthur Askey's memorial service, read:

The other career — author

*Dear Dickie*
*I very rarely write to famous people... that's*
*why I'm writing to you.*

*I would just like to say that I thought you*
*were superb the other day and I am sure that*
*Big Arthur would have been proud of you.*
*You made us all realise what a great loss we*
*have suffered and at the same time you made*
*us all happy.*

*Your tribute to Arthur reminded us all of*
*what a great comedian he was. I should like*
*to book you for mine, work permitting, just to*
*remind everyone what a great comedian I*
*was.*

*I would like to be cremated and my*

*favourite music is 'Smoke Gets in Your Eyes'.*

*PS: I'll pay you when I see you – down there!*

*PPS: I caught a glimpse of Dickie Murdoch*
*during the service and thought for one*
*horrible moment you might have to do a*
*second spot!*

☆

I was on holiday and not able to go to Eric's
funeral, but Dickie told me that he had read
this letter to the hundreds of mourners in
the church and the thousands overflowing
in the environs of Harpenden, and Eric

# Fiona Collier

Fiona Collier, née Webb, is a family friend from way back.

I always remember my mother telling me about going up to London in the same car as Eric, and just roaring with laughter the whole way.

Not too long after that, my sister Louise and I suffered the tragic loss of our parents and a younger sister in a helicopter accident. I was seventeen and Louise nineteen. Our lives were shattered.

A month or two after the tragedy, Eric and his son Gary and another friend came to our house for supper. I very much remember Eric's sensitivity in such harrowing circumstances, and just gently chatting about nothing in particular. He wasn't telling riproaring jokes or even just his quick little one-liners. He was actually quite serious. His face always made me laugh, especially the way he wriggled his nose which pushed up his glasses.

After dinner we went into the sitting-room and played a game of backgammon. It wasn't a late evening. After a few coffees and brandies, everyone left. I remember so vividly Eric as he left the house. As he walked out the door, he did that little jump as if someone had goosed him. He looked back at me as he did it, and I found that very funny. I smiled at him and he smiled back. He could almost have been hugging me in a way. There was something very caring about it all. What on earth could he have put into words to comfort a seventeen-year-old whose life had been so terribly shattered?

If he had made me laugh all evening – as he had with my mother – that would have been wrong. But to make me just smile said a lot and showed a very sensitive, caring and thoughtful side of him.

# David Benson

The actor, writer and director David Benson found fame and acclaim for his play about Kenneth Williams, which he wrote, starred in and directed. Benson is a lifelong fan of Eric Morecambe, and in the following anecdote describes their one meeting.

I was at a bookshop where Eric was doing a book-signing for his latest novel, *Mr Lonely*. I was really keen to get an autograph, but I didn't have enough money to buy the book. In the shop there were some cheaper paperback versions of the Morecambe and Wise Special, which I could just about afford.

I bought this cheaper book and queued to get Eric's inscription. When I finally got to him, I asked if he minded signing the paperback, and explained that I didn't have enough money to buy his new hardback release. He said he didn't mind at all, and signed my book. When I got outside I opened it up and saw what he'd written: 'To David, SAVE UP! Eric Morecambe'.

Needless to say, I have the book to this day.

# John Thaw

The actor John Thaw, famous for his roles in several major television series, including *Inspector Morse*, remembers Eric very well. Not only did he and Dennis Waterman – his fellow *Sweeney* star – appear on a Morecambe and Wise Christmas Show, but in return, Eric and Ernie were invited to appear in an episode of *The Sweeney*.

When I appeared on *The Morecambe and Wise Show*, I was struck by Eric's professionalism. He absolutely insisted on rigorous rehearsals. And the thing that sticks in my mind about those rehearsals is when Eric added an idea for a joke one day, and then cut it the next. He said, 'I'm cutting that laugh because we've got too many.' I remember thinking that was ridiculous, because that line had me in stitches. But he was adamant. He felt there were too many laughs in that particular sequence, which upset the balance, and he was cutting it.

Eric told me that his problem for years had been scripts – that the bane of his life was finding the right material. He was fed up with having to regurgitate material he'd been doing ten years earlier – it was basically the same stuff, even though it was

# Robert Lindsay

Robert Lindsay is one of our most popular actors. On stage and screen, his talent encompasses sit-com, musical theatre and Shakespearian tragedy.

coming from different writers. He said it was wearing him out.

He used to rewrite everything. Even when he and Ernie appeared on *The Sweeney* he took away the script and rewrote it. I believe if someone had come up to him with the offer of a more serious project, he'd have grabbed their hands off just to have had the chance of working on something fresh.

The other thing I recall about that *Sweeney* episode was that Billy Marsh, their agent, insisted they must have a caravan each on location. Thames asked what kind of caravan they'd like. They didn't really know, so Eric said they'd have whatever Dennis and myself usually used.

Now, on *The Sweeney*, we didn't have anything. We changed in cars or public lavatories and got made up in the backs of pubs. When he found that out, Eric said, 'We can't come on to a set and have a bloody great caravan each when the two stars are getting made up in a toilet round the back.' He insisted that if they had a caravan, we had to have one as well.

And that was the only time in four years on *The Sweeney* that Dennis and I had a caravan.

Christmas has lost its meaning since we lost Eric and Ernie. I was not fortunate enough to work with the greatest comic duo there has ever been, but I was lucky enough to meet them – or rather stand in their company – in the Light Entertainment Bar at the BBC. They had just finished recording a show and were surrounded by their many colleagues and admirers. I had just recorded an episode of *Citizen Smith* and I was surrounded by my agent. I managed to catch Eric's eye momentarily and raised my glass. He looked over his glasses, peered in my direction and, raising his glass, turned to Ernie and said, 'They let anyone in here now.'

# Peter Alliss

The former professional golfer Peter Alliss is now universally known as a commentator on golf. Peter, who never met Eric, has a son, Gary, who was the pro at Hammonds End Golf Club, which adjoins Eric's Harpenden home. Though Eric was once an enthusiastic golfer, he gave up the game in the mid-seventies, deciding he preferred using the course and its abundant woods for his new hobby, bird-watching.

My son, Gary, recalls seeing Eric in Harpenden on a number of occasions when he liked people to know it was *him*.

One such occasion was when he was in a shop; I know not whether it was the butcher, the baker or the candlestick-maker. Eric had on one of his big caps, glasses and had his pipe going; it was wintertime, overcoat on, and nobody had taken any sort of notice; indeed, nobody knew it was him.

Suddenly, he did his little movement where it looks as if someone's touched him from behind, and he gave the quick look round, touch of the glasses and movement of the cap, and all at once the shop was alive with fun and laughter, which Eric was able to create wherever he went.

He was taken far too soon, but what wonderful memories he's left behind for his public.

# Leslie Thomas

The novelist Leslie Thomas came to fame and fortune through his hugely successful novel *The Virgin Soldiers*. He met Eric on several occasions.

# Lynda Bellingham

The stage and screen actress Lynda Bellingham saw, rather than met, Eric. She has since become a friend of Eric's widow, Joan.

The story I remember about Eric concerns an event of some kind at, I think, the Savoy Hotel in London. I had never met Eric and Ernie at that time, but I remember they were walking towards my wife, Diana, and myself, when Eric suddenly said to Ernie, 'There's that chap wot writes the books.' As we all know, they had a running gag in which Ernie was about to write a novel or a play. They both approached and more or less surrounded me, firing comedy questions on how I went about writing fiction. It was as hilarious as quite a lot of things they did on television.

I encountered Eric one day at Television Centre. Although I was an enormous fan of his, we hadn't been introduced so I didn't really know him. I was walking along a corridor and he was coming the other way. It was one of those occasions when you only register recognition of someone once they've passed you. I suddenly thought, 'That's Eric Morecambe!' I stopped and turned to look back at him – only to see that he had stopped and turned to look back at *me*.

The difference was that Eric was wiggling his glasses and grinning all over his face.

'Bet you feel stupid now' was all he said.

He laughed, turned and carried on along the corridor as though nothing had happened.

# Jimmy Hill

To many people, Jimmy Hill is the voice and face of football. He knew
Eric well, particularly during the seventies, when they linked up on
various charity issues, as Jimmy's memory bears out.

Eric generously had joined a few other entertainers and sportsmen to raise
money under the name of the Goaldiggers for the National Playing Fields
Association. We played the odd football match, one at Windsor, with the Duke
of Edinburgh (our coach) and Eric (our linesman) supporting us from the
touchline.

When the time came to present a cheque to HRH for the money we had
raised, he invited us to Buckingham Palace, and the BBC were to film the
event.

Eric and I represented the Goaldiggers in what could so easily have been a
lacklustre and certainly unentertaining event. Eric thought differently. As the
camera rolled, he commenced an inimitable piece of Morecambe business.

'Have you got the cheque?' he asked.

'No,' said I, which produced over a minute's worth of mime, searching
pockets, raising eyebrows in a way that only Eric could achieve. Catching the
spirit of fun, I too began to mime shock/horror at the loss of the cheque. HRH
roared his head off, which added to the fun and games, and the master of
comedy had magically turned what could so easily have been a boring piece of
celluloid into golden comedy.

■ (Gary: My abiding memory of the above event – I saw the film –
is of Eric and Jimmy doing the Morecambe and Wise skip-dance
across the lawns of the Palace, humming 'Bring Me Sunshine'.)

# Barry Norman

Film critic Barry Norman has spent the last quarter of a century entertaining us with his views on the latest big-screen releases. He met Eric several times, and appeared on a Morecambe and Wise show.

I didn't, alas, know Eric nearly as well as I should have liked and yet somehow I miss him still. He was one of those rare people in whose presence you felt that life was a much happier affair than you had hitherto believed.

I only worked with Eric and Ernie once – on that Christmas show in which I, and several others, sang (and danced to) 'There is Nothing Like a Dame'. What struck me was their consummate professionalism. Before and after rehearsals and recording they were both terrific fun – Eric particularly, because he had that rare and marvellous gift of being naturally funny. He simply made us all laugh without apparently trying. But when the work started, the larking about stopped. They didn't waste time and they were amazingly patient with us blundering amateurs in the chorus, but they were quietly insistent that everything should be done right. Watching them, I realized that it was this striving for perfection, or as close to it as one could ever expect to get, that made them incomparably the greatest.

Some time later, when they'd gone to ITV, Eric asked if I would appear on one of the shows. I wanted to desperately, but the BBC – curse them! – said that if I did it would be an infringement of my contract. To this day I have never forgiven the BBC for that.

Once, when I was playing cricket for the Lord's Taverners at Peterborough, Eric turned up during the tea interval. He wandered into the marquee and spotted me sitting there with my seventeen-year-old daughter, Samantha, and asked if he could join us.

Obviously, we were delighted – especially Sam, to whom Eric was a great hero. As he and I chatted, Sam was a little tongue-tied at first but then he turned to her and said, 'Are you married?' She laughed and said no, and he sighed and said, 'Well, I am. That's the story of my life. Whenever I meet a pretty girl, either she's married or I am.' Sam loved him from that moment on.

A little later the actor Robin Askwith came by with his girlfriend, a long-legged blonde in miniskirt and purple tights. They stopped to talk a moment then moved on. As they went away, Eric looked thoughtfully at the girlfriend's purple legs and said, 'She's got terrible heart trouble, that girl.'

Eric was a gem; a one-off. Actually, I think he was a comic genius, and to anyone who challenges that statement I would simply say, 'Name me one other comedian who comes anywhere near his class?' There's nobody.

# Robert Runcie

The former Archbishop of Canterbury met Eric on several occasions, and they developed a fond friendship.

As the new bishop of St Albans in about 1971, I went to take a Confirmation service at Aldenham School. I was very nervous and all dressed up in my new regalia with cope, mitre, pastoral staff and so forth.

We were crowded together in the chapel, and I was rather on top of the big congregation. I had hardly started to speak when I noticed on the front row the famous face of Eric Morecambe looking up with that unmistakable and quizzical smile of expectation on his face. I had had no warning of this, and I was quite daunted as I opened my mouth and gave an address. It seemed clear to me that here was a man gathering material.

After the service was over and the congregation all came out with their proud youngsters, including Gary, they had a handshake from the Bishop. I was still togged up and perspiring in my regalia. As Eric approached me, he stepped back slightly, still with the same quizzical expression, looked me up and down and said, 'Ooh, the wax works are lifelike around here.' Of course it broke the ice and we were friends for ever after.

On another occasion, he was very proud to have discovered that the clerical directory, which is used by all who seek information about the clergy, is called *Crockford's*. It is the name of the publisher and is the Church of England Who's Who.

Eric was a member of a gambling club called Crockfords. He met me at this dinner in Luton and said, 'You know I am a member of the club. It means I can go into any cathedral in the land which has begun to charge for entry. I simply flash my card and murmur, "Crockford," and of course they wave me in.' You need the facial expression and the amazingly quick way in which he flashed the card and said 'Crockford' to get the full measure of the fun of this story.

Sometimes Eric accompanied Joan when she came into St Albans – perhaps to shop. Eric would be dangerously left on his own in the charming, rather olde-worlde Cathedral Street, which runs close to the cathedral itself. In this street, which is mainly antiques dealers and the like, there was a ladies' hairdresser. As you passed, you would see these ladies under their drying helmets and reading copies of *Vogue* and the like. It always struck me as rather strange. Anyway, it was too much for Eric. He would go up to the window and pull extraordinary faces and put his fingers in his ears and waggle them at these hapless ladies. It was a good thing that the proprietor of the shop had a sense of humour, otherwise Eric might have been arrested for molestation. He became quite a figure as a face-puller in that establishment for a short time.

I knew the proprietor, and it was she who told me about Eric's visits. It is a good example of Eric never really being able to be trusted on his own without making fun of something or someone – including himself.

# Anthony Swainson

From 1972 to 1991 Anthony Swainson was director of the Lord's Taverners, a charitable organization accredited by the England and Wales Cricket Board as the official national charity for recreational cricket.

In 1977, Eric Morecambe took over the presidency of the Lord's Taverners from HRH Prince Charles. They had a luncheon at the Royal Lancaster Hotel in London. Eric was in great form, and kept us all, including Prince Charles, in fits of laughter. Eric called it 'The Morecambe and Wales Show', and persuaded the Prince to trip the light fantastic.

Eric was very proud of being asked to continue his presidency. It was a charity to which he had become very attached. Above all, he loved sporting his cricket tie as worn by famous England cricketers.

Eric created a precedent by becoming the first president in the history of the Lord's Taverners (founded in 1950) to serve for three consecutive years – or, as he put it, 'to achieve my hat-trick'. It was not done again until ten years later, when Tim Rice took over in 1988.

In the year of the Queen's silver jubilee, Royal Tunbridge Wells invited Morecambe and Wise to their town as a surprise celebration. I lived with my family in Tunbridge Wells, and was invited by Eric to attend their show in the Assembly Hall.

We called at the stage door before the show. Eric was sitting in his dressing-room in a pair of Y-fronts, reading the *Fishing Times*. The dressing-room was typical of a provincial town; bare and unattractive. But Eric's presence and a bottle of whisky transformed the place into a five-star hotel. Such was the enjoyment and laughter that Eric almost forgot he was on stage in ten minutes.

The speed of his professional transformation was remarkable. Limbering-up exercise, make-up from a cigar box containing greasepaint, and the donning of his stage apparel hanging from a single hook on a brick wall.

Eric kindly arranged to have us seated in the wings. Each time his dance routine with Ernie brought him to our side of the stage, he gave us a broad wink and a sunshine smile.

Needless to say, the show was an enormous success. My wife and I and our daughter, Caroline, were privileged to have been Eric's guests.

# David Pleat

David Pleat is director of football at Tottenham Hotspur. For many years, he was manager of Luton Town Football Club. Having established that fact, little else needs to be said, except, perhaps, that yes, Eric was a director of the club during David's tenure.

I have many recollections of Eric. In the mid-seventies, when Luton won promotion to the First Division with a final win at West Bromwich Albion, Eric came into the dressing-room with great elation to congratulate the lads. Within seconds he was thrown into the bath, fully clothed and with his glasses on. He was more worried about losing his glasses than about getting soaked and having to travel back down the motorway in borrowed clothes. His glasses were his treasured prop.

At Luton, we were always looking for ways of raising funds to keep the club going. We looked at sponsorship for everything. At a board meeting there were several complaints that had arisen because the railway line that ran alongside the back of the ground was only used once a day by a train carrying materials to Sundon, and it was getting very unsightly. It seemed the whole of Luton was dumping rubbish there, and VIPs and season-ticket-holders entering the ground by the back entrance had to walk right past this unsightly mess.

It was suggested that we put up high corrugated-metal sheets against the fence so people could not see the railway line. When the chairman said we could not afford to buy the corrugated sheets, Eric at once volunteered to sponsor one of them.

Eric was always smiling, and you would never ever catch him in a serious mood, whatever his own or any family circumstances might have been at the that time.

He would come into the dressing-room before games to lighten the tension, making faces, telling tales or larking around. Before one of the games we all decided that, whatever hilarity he attempted, the players would keep a straight face and not move a muscle. No one was even to look at him. He left the room promptly that day with his tail between his legs, but knowing within seconds that the players had generated this collusion.

One afternoon after a reserve game at Luton, Eric and I were sharing a pot of coffee. He suggested I experiment with holding up boards with a letter or figure on them during the games, which would signify a tactic to use. When I held the board aloft, the players would know which plan to use, similar to the American Football game.

I didn't have the heart to tell him that many of the players would pretend that they couldn't see the boards and those that could wouldn't remember what the signal represented.

*Eric and Gary at Morecambe F.C., 1969*

# Jonathan Pryce

Actor Jonathan Pryce has a successful and varied career. He reached an international audience through appearances in such films as *Evita* and *Tomorrow Never Dies*. He was, and is, a huge fan of Morecambe and Wise.

I've loved the duo since seeing them live in Liverpool in the early seventies. They were wonderful on that stage. What I particularly enjoyed was seeing the variety-hall material and approach to their work as opposed to the more familiar television material and approach.

The best review I ever had came early in my career when I was playing Tranio in *The Taming of the Shrew* in Nottingham in 1974: I was described as 'Eric Morecambe in full flight'. I wouldn't say I'd played the role as Eric, but I had embodied the spirit of the clown in the way that he always did.

Eric and I met twice. The first, as I imagine with many, was in a lift at the BBC. It was one of those moments when you felt you knew him because you recognized him, so you say the big hello, then think, 'Jesus, but I *don't* know him.'

The second occasion was at an event at the New London Theatre, this being before *Cats* had opened. I knew a fashion designer called Pauline, who was showing clothes at an exhibition running there. Across the foyer, much to my delight, stood Eric Morecambe.

I was having a drink with my partner, Kate, when Eric came up to me. 'Hello Jon, how are you? What are you doing these days?' All this sort of stuff. I was struck dumb. It transpired that Pauline had set it up. She had gone over to Eric and said what a huge fan of his I was, and would he mind coming over for a chat.

The great thing about Eric was that you cared about him – felt you knew him personally. He touched people's lives.

# Joanna Lumley

Eric always liked Joanna Lumley and was keen to have her on the show. He was impressed by her grace and comic timing, and would not have been surprised by her success as Patsy in *Absolutely Fabulous*. A little like her alter ego, Joanna was rather 'dizzy' at the time we approached her with various work-related distractions, but in a fax sent to Martin she did remark that 'I adored being with Eric and Ernie – Eric was a genius – and a *fab* dancer!'

# Peter Bowles

The actor Peter Bowles, who seems to have appeared in just about everything on television – including *The Morecambe and Wise Show* – has fond memories of time spent with Eric and Ernie.

Apart from the friendliness and fun I had in Eric and Ernie's company, the only particular memory is that during rehearsals, including the final camera rehearsal at the studio, all sorts of lines, jokes and cues were thrown at me. (I was a psychiatrist, with Eric and Ernie facing me.)

When we came to the actual take, I heard the scripted lines for the first time, delivered with Eric's tremendous timing and confidence – and I was electrified into changing up three gears just to keep with them.

After the take, I discovered they had had all their lines written up on a board directly behind my head – but the ad-libbed rehearsals had been fun.

# Donald Sinden

The actor of stage, film and television knew and worked with Eric. The following anecdotes concern Donald's son, Jeremy, who tragically died of cancer in 1996.

Jeremy was in the regular cast of the TV serial *Crossroads* which was recorded in Birmingham. One night, Morecambe and Wise were also performing in Birmingham (this would be about 1980). Jeremy, who had often met them with me, went backstage after their performance. He told them he had just become a father to a baby girl.

'What name are you giving her?' asked Eric.

Jeremy explained, 'Years ago I saw the name Kezia inscribed on a tombstone in Norfolk and I said to myself that if I ever had a daughter, I'd call her that—'

Eric cut in: 'I like it – That Sinden!'

☆

Some years earlier, in a similar situation backstage in Birmingham (circa 1976), Eric asked Jeremy, 'What's your father up to?'

Jeremy replied, 'He's going to play King Lear at Stratford-upon-Avon.'

An astonished Eric asked, 'Have they told him?'

Not the reaction anyone would have expected.

■ (Gary: Eric loved to play with words in his gagging. '*That* Sinden' reminds me of the time I introduced him to a rather attractive friend. 'Who is she?' he asked. 'Just a friend,' I casually replied. A couple of months later, the same friend, who had a poster of Eric and Ernie, asked Eric to sign it. He signed it: 'To a friend – just!' How he remembered the conversation of before still bemuses me.)

# Jeremy Beadle

Television presenter Jeremy Beadle met Eric several times, and recalls some wonderful moments in his company.

*Game for a Laugh* was a rare event in television: a hole in one. Within a few weeks of the first transmission, I found myself sitting on the top table at a huge showbiz charity function. All the great names of comedy were in the room, and I had the wonderful privilege of having Ernie on my left and Eric on my right. Halfway through the evening, I said to Eric, 'I don't know what I'm doing here at the top table. I've only been in the business five minutes,' to which Eric replied, 'Don't knock it. They may not ask you back next year.' In fact, they didn't ask me back for *eight* years.

On another occasion, after I had just been punished by some particularly vitriolic criticism in the press, Eric comforted me with the words 'Don't worry, Jeremy. The hardest thing to find in a home is yesterday's newspaper.'

One of the last occasions I was with Eric, I asked him if he would appear on a television pilot I was presenting. I asked him to give me his five funniest silent-screen moments. He said he would love to, especially as it would be so easy: all five clips would be from Buster Keaton films. Then, for the next forty minutes, he gave me a unique masterclass in the theory of comedy, explaining why each clip was so brilliant. I sat and listened in awe as one of the great comic geniuses paraded forth his ideas on what makes people laugh. It remains one of the greatest moments of my life to have been given the privilege of hearing the best from the finest.

# Freddy Trueman

The renowned former England fast bowler Freddy Trueman met Eric on many occasions.

I first met Eric in Australia in the late fifties, when I was touring with England. I was immediately taken with his wonderful humour. I did not know at the time that I was in the presence of a comic genius to be: some of his off-the-cuff remarks make me titter to this day.

When he was president of the Lord's Taverners, he spoke at the spring lunch. This was the year after Brian Close had been battered black and blue by Hall and Griffiths in the test match at Lord's. There were bruises all over his body; he looked like a leopard. There was a saying in cricket for many years: 'The sound of leather on willow, now that summer is here'. In his opening remarks, Eric said, 'I knew the cricket season had started when I heard the sound of leather on Closey.' He brought the house down, including HRH The Duke of Edinburgh.

☆

Another memory is of Eric having his ear bashed about show business by some know-it-all, who, after a long explanation, said, 'You see, Eric, in comedy you need three things.' Before he could proceed further, Eric replied with what I consider to be a cracking rejoinder: 'If you have three things, you should be in a circus.'

Wonderful.

# Fred Rumsey

Former England cricketer Fred Rumsey was a long-time friend of Eric.

As a former test cricketer, I slipped very easily into the body of Eric's friends – a motley crowd, mostly from show business and sport. This fact, his love for sport and his dedication to charity, eventually led him into the ranks of the Lord's Taverners; and it was at one of their many dinner functions that our paths first crossed. It is fair to say that I had been a fan of Eric's for many years, but what I did not know was that he had never heard of me. At that time, Eric was one of the best after-dinner speakers making the rounds, though in his case it was mostly for fun and charity. The fact that his presentation was short, to the point and funny gave rise to little criticism.

We all abuse our friends a little, and it was in this area of personal appearance that I gently abused Eric. I liked Eric a lot, and I also liked to be known as the man who was a friend of Eric Morecambe. Whenever he visited me in Derbyshire, I would throw a little soirée to introduce him to my local friends and acquaintances. On one such occasion, we had spent the whole day fly-fishing on the Wye and the Derwent, arriving back after the party had started. True to form, Eric wasted no time and immediately set about entertaining the gathering with his usual wit and charm. At about 11.30 p.m. a tired-looking Eric took me to one side asking me to call an end to the proceedings. Knowing that we were off fishing again at the break of dawn, and respecting his wishes, I did so. My wife, Coleen, began to batten down the hatches, and Eric called for a final night-cap. Two other friends were spending the night with us, and the five of us relaxed with what I incorrectly thought was going to be our last drink. From that moment on, Eric re-enacted the whole day's fishing, finding humour in situations that had simply passed me by. For two and a half hours, he had us laughing until our sides were fit to burst. There was no stealing from past scripts, or the sometimes boring repetition of catch-phrases; just humour based on the day's events. When he eventually finished, possibly out of exhaustion, a wide grin spread across his face. 'You know,' he said, 'I got more pleasure out of that, making you – my friends – laugh, than I get out of all the professional appearances I make.'

In 1976, Brian Close, then captain of Somerset County Cricket Club, asked me to arrange two fund-raising dinners for his benefit or testimonial. Having made the basic arrangements and selected the venues, one in Bristol, the other in Derby, I

Ernie has lost his wallet
somewhere...

started looking at organizing the entertainment. Fortunately, Eric was prepared to attend both events, and I decided on a forum as the most comfortable mode to present him. When the publicity for the Derby event advertised the fact that Brian Close, Hedley Muscroft, Brian Clough and Ted Moult would join Eric on the forum, we had a sell-out.

A Derby builder, a man I knew very well, asked me if any of the celebrities attending would be prepared to officially open one of his commercial building-sites. I asked him, 'Which one – celebrity, that is?' Looking at me sideways, he said, 'You don't suppose Eric would do it, do you?' 'I'll ask him,' I told him.

Eric accepted, and the morning after the forum we both presented ourselves to the site where, at my request, a large hole had been dug.

'What are we doing with that?' asked Eric.

'I don't know,' I replied. 'You're the celebrity; *you* decide.'

'Thanks very much, Sunshine,' he retorted. 'That's another hole you've got me into.'

To assist the builder, I had asked the local TV station to attend. They jumped at the chance of interviewing Eric. 'Mr Morecambe, can you tell us why you're down a hole, in the middle of an empty field, here in Derbyshire?'

'I've heard there's water here,' replied Eric (at this time the country was in drought). 'No, I lie,' he said. 'Ernie has lost his wallet somewhere in this area, and there is a million-pound reward on offer. The only condition is that you give the remainder back.'

If anything, the dinner in Bristol was more successful than the one in Derby. This time the panel consisted of Eric, Brian Close and Ed Stewart. Just before the forum was due to start, a famous TV actor presented himself at my table, explaining that he was staying in the hotel, had heard about the event and wondered if he could join me. Although he was not in DJ, he was not going to be seen by many, so I agreed to let him stay. Halfway through the forum, he was suddenly on his feet for all to see. 'My question,' he said in a pompous voice, 'is directed at Mr Morecambe. Why have I never received an invitation to appear on your Christmas Show?'

Quick as a flash, Eric replied, 'First of all, Sunshine, you don't know how to dress properly and, secondly, you might accept.'

Immediately following the dinner, a Swindon businessman approached me, asking if Eric would consider opening a home-improvement centre in that town. I suggested that we spoke to Eric together, and again Eric agreed.

This time the centre was already constructed, so there was no need for holes. The TV crews came along, as usual, and Eric gave his normal polished interviews.

# Russ Abbot

The comedian Russ Abbot met Eric on a couple of occasions and professes to be one of his greatest fans.

During one, he grabbed a little boy from a group of watchers and created a sketch by getting the boy to ask the questions after he, Eric, had already answered them. When the cameras had left, I accused him of making every situation a sketch – he did not deny it.

Talking about sketches reminded him of Ann Hamilton, an actress who appeared in the sketches 'wot' he and Ernie wrote. Ann was running a theatre in Swindon at the time, and he insisted that I join him to meet her and have a cup of tea. Tea seemed a pleasant change from the celebratory fare we had been consuming, so I agreed to go along. Clive Dunn was appearing at the theatre at that time, so he joined us for a very pleasant interlude.

After tea, Ann conducted Eric and me to the theatre to have a look. It was in the form of an amphitheatre with the seats stretching from where we were standing at the back of the theatre straight down to the stage, with no orchestra pit.

Ann said, 'You can whisper a line at the back of the stage and be heard throughout the theatre.'

'Pardon?' said Eric.

I was doing a stage show, and afterwards I heard that Eric Morecambe was coming backstage to visit me. My young son was there, and earlier that day he had bought himself a shiny leather suit which went from neck to toe.

Eric came into the dressing-room, shook hands with me, glanced at my son and said, 'I see you've brought your wallet.'

# Bob 'The Cat' Bevan

Comedian, entertainer and king of after-dinner speaking, Bob Bevan is particularly well known to members and friends of the Lord's Taverners. He has described Eric as one of his major heroes.

When I had a 'proper' job, I was head of public relations for European Ferries. During this time, I approached Jimmy Savile about using Townsend Thoresen car ferries for one of his programmes. As a result of this, we became good friends. He knew I hero-worshipped Morecambe and Wise, and one day he telephoned to tell me that they were to appear on *Jim'll Fix It*. If I would like to come up to the studio, he would introduce me to them.

When I arrived at Television Centre, Jim took me into their dressing-room, and we had a long chat. They both seemed very pleasant chaps. Ernie told me that he was very familiar with Townsend Thoresen ships, as he was a shareholder in order to get the discount. Eric said, 'You would be.' Obviously the joke was true!

Ernie then told me how well he was looked after on the ships, but that come what may he could not avoid the fans. He said that he had recently come back from Cherbourg and a little boy had followed him around awestruck at seeing him in the flesh. Eventually, Ernie told him that he was going to his cabin for a sleep and that maybe he should keep watch outside the door, assuming that the kid would soon get bored and leave. Ernie actually went to sleep; he woke up a couple of hours later to find, to his acute embarrassment, that the boy was still outside the door keeping watch. A conscience-stricken Ernie had to take him to the bar and buy him several Cokes.

I finally got to work on the same bill as Eric in the year that he died. In May, 1984, I was the 'turn' at the *Sunday People* Football Merit Awards on the night before the Cup Final. During the evening, Eric was called up on stage to present one of the awards. Called up next to join him was Kevin Keegan. Without mentioning Kevin's name, Eric said to him, 'I've always admired you and I wondered if you'd give me your autograph for my son.' He then produced a scrap of paper and handed it to Kevin. Kevin took out a pen and signed this piece of paper. Eric took the paper back. Then he screwed it up and threw it away over his shoulder. It was one of the funniest visual wind-ups I have ever seen, and quite typical of Eric.

# Paul Daniels

Magician, presenter and comedian Paul Daniels has been entertaining the nation for... well, surely for ever. He is a great admirer of Eric Morecambe, and the two men met many times.

I was in a nightclub in Grays, Essex. So were many other stars, including Cliff (now Sir Cliff) Richard; and, as the event was in the presence of HRH Prince Charles, of course Eric and Ernie were there, they being firm royal favourites. How the club organized this lot to come to their smoky den I have no idea. Cliff was to do the cabaret later, and we were all sitting round a table having dinner. Being fairly new to the scene I was, quite rightly, sitting at one end, boggled at the fact that I was so close to the gods of show business.

Typical of nightclubs, it was quite dark and very noisy, which covered up what happened next. Eric stood up from centre table and set off to go to the toilets. As he rounded the corner of the table where I was sitting, he got hold of my hair, lifting the edge in the same way that he got hold of Ernie's in every show, and came out with the catch-phrase 'Way-hey, you can't see the join, you know' – just as he always pretended that Ernie had a wig – and sailed onwards.

As he came back round the corner of the table, I caught his jacket and pulled him down. 'That could have been very embarrassing.'

In my ear he whispered, 'It was – I didn't know you wore one,' and he walked away. The response was so fast that I collapsed laughing.

■ (Gary: Paul once told me that he had to stop watching my father on television because he, Paul, found himself copying the style and the timing and he was in danger of becoming a second Eric Morecambe. 'Now, I could quite happily have coped with becoming the *first* Eric Morecambe.')

# Magdi Yacoub

Magdi Yacoub came to prominence through his pioneering work in heart bypass surgery. After Eric suffered his second coronary in 1979, he was referred to Yacoub at Harefield Hospital, where the world-renowned heart specialist is based.

Eric really thought about every little detail in everything he did. That called on all his reserves, and that had an effect on his heart. Many people tried to advise him to retire but I didn't think that was a good idea. I thought that he should not stop, merely modify his way of doing things. But that was impossible for Eric.

■ (Gary: On their first meeting, Magdi Yacoub said to Eric and Joan, 'We've looked at all the evidence and seen the results of the tests, and my recommendation is that you should have a bypass operation.'

'What would happen if I didn't have the operation?' asked Eric.

'Then I wouldn't expect you to live more than a few months,' replied Yacoub.

'What are you doing this afternoon?' asked Eric.)

# Kenneth Williams

Kenneth Williams was one of the most original and distinctive comedians of the twentieth century. This stalwart of the *Carry On* film series was, initially, no fan of either Eric or Ernie. He describes them as his 'least favourite comics' in an entry in his diaries, published in 1993.

Curiously he did enjoy their second film, *That Riviera Touch*. 'There were some very original things in this film,' he said, 'which was very well done. These two came out of it very well indeed – very much "innocents abroad" and at times a real note of pathos was established.'

Some years later, in the early 1980s, Williams appeared on a radio programme with both Eric and Ernie and redressed his earlier diary entry with a more positive one:

'They have a fundamental honesty and goodness which probably accounts for their universal popularity.'

# Roy Hudd

Comedian and broadcaster Roy Hudd has enjoyed a long and successful career.

I had never met Eric Morecambe. I, like most other lesser mortals, merely worshipped from afar. Then, one winter afternoon, I came up the steps from Piccadilly Circus Underground station with my suit-bag over my arm. I was bound for rehearsals for a BBC Radio variety show at their Lower Regent Street studio.

As I came into the daylight, an oh-so-familiar voice said, 'Aha! Who's off to do a radio show, then?' It was the great man himself. He too had a suit-bag over one arm. 'I've just done one,' he said. 'Look.' He waved his suit-bag at me. 'Do you realize we are the only two comics who get dressed up for a *radio* show?' Then he was gone.

I still cherish that word 'we'.

*Eric and Ernie with Tony Curtis while filming in the South of France in the mid-60s*

Two familiar faces in the crowd

# Mark Stuart

Mark Stuart, producer and director at Thames Television, produced *The Morecambe and Wise Show* circa 1980.

I inherited *The Morecambe and Wise Show* from the distinguished producer John Ammonds.

John had worked with 'the boys' – as they were always known – for many years and had built up a very special relationship with them. This meant they were more or less 'house-trained', or so I thought. 'Give us a director who will stand up to us,' they had told Philip Jones, 'someone who will fight us for what he wants, who will argue with us when he thinks we are wrong and, of course, will do exactly what we tell him to do.'

On this uneasy basis we began a series in which we fought not at all, argued occasionally and laughed a great deal.

Rehearsals with the 'big name' guests were always a joy. Performers of vast experience in their own field would come to rehearsals with the wary, expectant look of children arriving at a party. They need not have worried. Usually in a matter of moments Eric and Ernie had relaxed them and got them deeply involved in the exact science of throwing a custard pie or learning a dance step while wearing a full suit of armour.

Sir Ralph Richardson had some reservations. 'I only want to do the bit I've agreed to be in,' he said. 'I don't want to make a fool of myself or do anything silly.'

'Of course, Sir Ralph,' we said.

'And by the way, I would quite like to do that little dance at the end wearing an old mac and carrying a paper bag.'

'Nothing silly?' we said.

'No,' he said.

'Of course,' we said.

# Judi Dench

Judi Dench's highly acclaimed performances have ranged from her Oscar-winning Elizabeth I in *Shakespeare in Love* to James Bond's boss, M, and from a tour de force in David Hare's play *Amy's View* to the cosy TV sit-com *As Time Goes By*. She appeared on *The Morecame and Wise Show* in 1978.

Eric was like Billy Connolly in our house. They are the only two performers we, as a family, would ever cancel everything to watch. So when I was invited to appear on one of the Morecambe and Wise shows at Thames Television, I was frightened. In fact, absolutely terrified.

But I needn't have worried because as soon as I got to rehearsals I found I was in safe hands. You see, although it looked to the audience as though Eric was ad-libbing all the time, he was actually meticulous in rehearsal about timing every laugh and every line. I know it might surprise some people to learn that he was extremely masterful: he was the one who really drove those shows.

I learnt so much from him, particularly comic timing. He even taught me how to do that famous paper-bag trick of his: the one where he throws an imaginary ball into the air and pretends to catch it. I still do it all the time.

When we were rehearsing the show, Eric admired a pen I had. So, as a thank you to him and Ernie, I bought an identical one for each of them. When I gave Eric his pen, he said, 'I'm really touched. That's beautiful. I'm going to treasure that for the rest of my life.' He then walked away and pretended to throw it away over his shoulder. That made me laugh so much. Again, it's a gag of his I've pinched and repeat to this day.

After I appeared on *The Morecambe and Wise Show*, Eric and his wife, Joan, became such good, sweet friends: Joan is a genuinely delightful person. They came to dinner on one occasion and I was serving salmon. And, would you believe, the hollandaise sauce curdled just as I heard them arrive.

Eric walked in and said to me, 'Hello, young man, what's for supper?'

'Salmon,' I said.

'In that case, I'll just have the vegetables.'

I thought he'd seen the sauce and was joking. But, for once, he was being serious. It turned out that he'd eaten so much salmon at various lunches and dinners recently, that he was sick of it.

Next time he came to dinner, though, he brought me a big salmon, which he'd caught himself, because he had remembered my saying how much I love it. That was so typical of his thoughtfulness.

On another occasion, he came to dinner and brought us a bottle of vintage champagne, which I put in the fridge. During the meal, there was an almighty crash from the kitchen. I hurried through to find out what disaster had befallen us and found that my daughter's nanny had opened the fridge door, unaware that the champagne was there. Of course, the bottle had rolled out and smashed on the floor. I was mortified, and the nanny and I stood there consoling each other. I didn't know what on earth I could say to Eric about shattering his lovely gift.

'What smashed in the kitchen?' he asked when I returned to the table.

'That's for you to guess,' I said, playing for time.

'The pudding?'

Eric was truly unique. A lovely, lovely man with a heavenly talent whom I adored. He literally made me cry with laughter and taught me so much about comedy. I was devastated when he died.

# Harry Fowler

The actor Harry Fowler began his career in films in the 1940s; his many TV appearances include the hit sit-com *The Army Game*. He was the guest star on the penultimate Morecambe and Wise TV show, broadcast in October 1983.

I spent a week rehearsing at the Richmond Rugby Club (used by Thames as rehearsal rooms) for the *Morecambe and Wise Show* back in the mid-eighties.

Eric, next to Peter Noble, was the walking encyclopaedia on the character performers in late-pre-war, wartime, and postwar black-and-white American, as well as British, films.

Each morning I'd turn up with a name to fox him, like Elisha Cook Jr or Victor Sen Yung (Charlie Chan's second son). All were too easy for him.

The final morning, I confronted him with Nehemiah Persoff. It took him a good half-hour before – having finished a quick sketch run-through – he came over, unlit pipe at the 'gottit' angle, and said, 'Mr Persoff. He played, among many other roles, Johnny Torio in *Al Capone*.'

A top movie buff.

Eric and Ernie with Harry Fowler

We also shared stories of our times working in the coalmines (not the same one). Like him, I was conscripted during the war into the Bevin Boy scheme. It was definitely worth having done, we both agreed. It made you appreciate the jobs *above* ground. And the more especially, show business.

Nigel Hawthorne in the Sherlock Holmes sketch

# Nigel Hawthorne

Nigel Hawthorne became a household name for his portrayal of Whitehall mandarin Sir Humphrey Appleby in the TV series *Yes, Minister* and *Yes, Prime Minister*. He found international fame with his portrayal of George III in the film version of Alan Bennett's play *The Madness of King George*. He met Eric on a number of occasions.

I was enormously flattered to have been asked to take part in *The Morecambe and Wise Show* during their time at Thames Television. In fact, I appeared twice. I think it was on the second of these occasions that Eric had a heart attack while recording a flicker flashback sequence.

Eric knew that he made me laugh. He also knew that I would come in early to rehearsal, when he and Ernie would stop what they were doing, plonk me down as an audience, and run through for me all the stuff they had been rehearsing. After lunch they would stay on in the bar until chuck-out time, talking about the old days. I felt enormously privileged to be included.

When we were doing the Sherlock Holmes sketch, Eric asked if I would come to his birthday party. When I asked when that was, he told me it was almost a year

hence. To be frank, I forgot all about it. Out of the blue, Thames Television rang months later, saying, was I coming? Eric wanted to know.

I took a bottle of champagne round to the rehearsal room where Eric, Ernie and Roy Castle were having a lunch break. Patricia Brake (who played the maid in the Sherlock Holmes sketch) and I were the only other birthday guests.

In the Sherlock Holmes sketch there was a song and dance. The reader may recall that the set featured a large gorilla. Its arms could be moved (and were) by Eric. Just before the final dress run, the choreographer took me on one side and explained that at the end of the dance, when we all went off, the door was at such an angle that the camera could only see our disappearing backs. He asked that I, being the last, should stop, turn and execute a few steps facing front before joining the others.

The final dress run went remarkably well. My desperate attempts to dance evoked cheers and applause from everybody around. Through the hubbub I heard Eric's voice: 'Instead of that, we'll cut to the gorilla.' I realized that I was encroaching on the comedians' territory. I was there as the straight man, and I had been firmly put in my place. It was a most valuable lesson.

# Chris Tarrant

Television and radio presenter Chris Tarrant vividly remembers meeting Eric.

The Morecambe and Wise Christmas shows were an essential ingredient of my growing up – as much a part of my Christmas as turkey and the Queen's speech. In fact, to be truthful, I probably slept through a lot of Her Majesty's best speeches, but I never, ever slept when Eric and Ernie were on. They were absolutely magnificent, attracting audiences that no shows have ever attracted since – even the repeats remain hugely watchable.

The banter between Eric and long-suffering little Ern, the glasses, the cheek-slapping, the catch-phrases like 'Ready when you are, Sunbeam', the guests like Angela Rippon, Glenda Jackson, Shirley Bassey and, of course, the ludicrous dance off at the end, somehow all combined to make one of the greatest television shows of my lifetime. It was nonsense, it was slapstick and it looked very ad-lib, although it certainly wasn't because Eric was a total professional about everything he did; and it was good clean family fun.

Isn't it strange that in those days we thought there was nothing remotely suspect about two grown men not just sharing a house together, but sharing a double bed. It was all done in a spirit of total innocence, and it was exactly the same with

Eric (back row, far left) playing football with Stan Stennett
(front row, left with son) and Alan Curtis (third from right, top row)

# Stan Stennett

Stan Stennett first worked with Eric and Ernie on a radio show in Manchester in the early 1950s. It was at Stan's theatre in Tewkesbury that, in May 1984, Eric collapsed and died, following an on-stage interview in front of a large audience.

Eric and Ernie were very, very funny on the radio, and everyone thought it was simply a question of moving that format over to television. But life isn't always quite as easy as that, which is why *Running Wild*, their first series, was a flop. That series gave them a few rough years, because it nearly broke them and put a temporary halt to their rise to stardom.

Eric was appearing in a charity show for me at the Roses Theatre, Tewkesbury. The place was packed and when he joined me on the stage the audience fell apart. We talked about the people we'd met and worked with. We talked about Diana Dors, a mutual friend, who'd just passed away, and inevitably we moved on to Tommy Cooper, who'd also died a couple of months earlier.

'When I go, I hope I don't die in front of an audience,' Eric said.

He kept pulling things out of the past that even I, who'd known him over thirty

years, didn't recognize. It's like that old gag about the drowning man going down for the third time who has enjoyed his past life flashing by so much that he decides to go down again. Eric talked a lot about his childhood and how he started as a comedian. So it could well be that he was having some kind of premonition of his own death on that stage and felt compelled to talk about his own past.

Eventually, we came to the end of the evening, as we thought. He got up, took his applause and then went into 'Bring Me Sunshine'. Then, as a tribute to him, we played 'The Entertainer'. He came on again, joined in and suddenly it all went up a gear.

He went off to the side of the stage, said, 'Thank God that's over,' to his chauffeur, Mike, and then collapsed.

We asked if there was a doctor in the house, and the theatre went silent. It was as though everyone had become mute. I went on and said, 'Well, ladies and gentlemen, the doctor's with him and we're going to get him to a hospital.' Then everyone just began to walk out of the theatre very slowly, zombie-like. It was the strangest thing one could ever imagine. It was as though they knew instinctively that something dreadful was about to happen.

# Christopher Biggins

The actor Christopher Biggins recalls
the time he unexpectedly met Eric.

I bumped into Eric and Ernie one day while I
was making *Poldark*. I got into a lift at the
studios and said a general 'Hello' to everyone
in it before I realised I was sharing it with
Morecambe and Wise. Now, Eric was my
absolute idol. I'd grown up with him in my
sitting-room, like everyone else, and it was just
great to meet him – albeit unexpectedly.

But he was so sweet, because before I could
start stammering how delighted I was to meet
him, he suddenly started saying what a
pleasure it was to meet me and how much he
loved me in *Poldark*. He really put me at my
ease: I was on cloud 9. How typical of him to
turn a situation round like that.

Eric asked me to appear on *The Morecambe
and Wise Show*, and I would have dearly loved
to have done it. Alas, it wasn't to be, because
he died before we could arrange it.

# Christopher Thursby Pelham

The former director-general of the British Heart Foundation recalls
Eric casting a fishing-line.

Probably my happiest recollection of Eric Morecambe is of him casting a
line from a boat in St Katharine's Dock, then hooking and landing a
gumboot. The occasion was the launch of a nationwide sponsored angling
competition in aid of the British Heart Foundation; just one of the many
fund-raising events enhanced by his inimitable sense of humour. It was
only afterwards that I learnt he had a thorough dislike of water.

Eric's support for the BHF is now legendary. Over the years he gave
his time and talent to raise funds for the research work he believed in so
strongly. Not only did he attend fund-raising events both large and small,
but his photograph appeared in several of our campaigns.

One morning, a year before he died, he gave up some time to be
interviewed for the BHF's magazine, *Heart Bulletin*, and even took the
trouble to meet our editor at the station. His courage and humour were
always evident and a constant encouragement to others who suffered as he
did. He made light of his problems, even his first heart attack, about which
he said: 'I didn't know what was happening – I thought I'd got my braces
twisted at the back.'

That is how we like to remember him: a delightful man, a great and
loyal supporter of our work, and courageous to the end.

# Part 2

# Eric's legacy

And then there are those who never met Eric
but nevertheless wished to contribute to this
celebration of him.

# Paddy Ashdown

Former leader of the Liberal Democrats Paddy Ashdown regrets never having had the opportunity to meet Morecambe and Wise.

When my father came back from Australia after ten years of absence, and in the three years before he died in my house, we used to make watching Morecambe and Wise an almost religious event in our household. I laughed hugely at them myself. But I will never forget the joy that Eric Morecambe and his partner gave to my father in his last days.

# Cameron Mackintosh

Cameron Mackintosh is the producer of West End hit musicals such as *Les Misérables*.

My memory of them is the sheer joy of watching their Christmas specials and seeing some famous 'legit' performers being put through their paces. Sadly, I never met either of them or even saw them live on stage.

# William Hague

William Hague, Leader of the Opposition, was very young when Eric and Ernie were at their peak. Like many who grew up on the double act, he has very fond memories of them.

I am delighted to have been asked to contribute to a collection of reminiscences about the late Eric Morecambe. Eric was a British institution who had people in stitches the length and breadth of the country. I, like countless millions, looked forward each year to his and Ernie's Christmas special.

I'll always remember the moments when he would ask, 'What do you think of the show so far?' to which someone, or some*thing*, would pipe up 'Rubbish!' It often comes to mind during debates in Parliament.

For many years to come the mere mention of his name will be raising smiles all over the country. The laughter he brought to so many of our lives will not be forgotten.

# Dale Winton

Television presenter Dale Winton never met Eric, but knows his son Gary.

I attended Aldenham School in Hertfordshire with Gary, and I was very excited about my mother being in the show with Morecambe and Wise. They have always been the premium double-act – first-class and always funny. I remember when my mother was told by the make-up lady that she was not allowed to wear her false eyelashes on the show. She came home very upset, but she did win in the end.

■ (Gary: A few years ago, I bumped into Dale at an awards do at BBC Television Centre. Having totally forgotten that he'd also been at Aldenham, I went up to him and introduced myself: 'Hello, I'm Gary Morecambe.'

'Don't give me that "Morecambe" crap, Bartholomew,' replied Dale. 'We were in the same house at school together.')

Joan, Gary and Eric

# Jeremy Novick

Jeremy Novick, a journalist on the *Daily Express*, is also author of a book on Morecambe and Wise called *You Can't See the Join*.

For reasons that aren't relevant here – it's a long story – a few years ago I was walking across the brow of a mountain in Nepal with a friend called Cissi, a twenty-two-year-old Swedish woman.

It was a lovely place, full of other mountains and valleys and a river, and the like. But we had a lot of time on our hands and Cissi, bless her, loves to talk. So we started talking about our formative influences; things that we used to do; things that we used to watch. The subject of TV programmes came up. Cissi told me about a peace-loving bull called Ferdinand, who used to sit underneath trees and smell flowers and recite poetry.

I told her about Morecambe and Wise. I don't know whether it was because she was Swedish, or whether it was because she was only twenty-two, but she had about as much idea of Morecambe and Wise as I had about Ferdinand.

'Well, Eric was the tall balding one who used to move his glasses to the side of his face and tease the other one who had short, fat, hairy legs and say he couldn't see the join in his hairline...'

'He wore a wig?'

'No, it was all his own hair.'

'So what was the join he couldn't see?'

'Doesn't matter. Anyway, he would slap him round the face...'

'What? He would hit him?'

'No, no. They were best friends.'

'So why did he hit him? Did they have a fight?'

'No, forget it. It was just a slap round the face. They were friends, believe me. They used to live together. Some of the sketches they did were set in their double bed.'

'...?'

After a while I gave up trying to explain. Maybe you had to be there.

# Shaun Prendergast

Actor and writer Shaun Prendergast is a lifelong fan of
Eric Morecambe.

One of the first jobs I had as an actor was as a member of the Radio
Drama Company and one of the first gigs I did was a play in
Manchester. Although I'd known the city as a student it was the first
time I'd worked there as a pro, and I was thrilled to be staying at the
house of the legendary theatrical landlady Mrs McKay.

When I met her, she was brusque, direct and a dead ringer for Thora
Hird. I sat, wide-eyed, leafing through the ancient visitors' books that
had been signed by all of her guests.

'Frank Randall?' I gasped.

She nodded briskly. 'Terrible man. Used to take his teeth out and
break wind on stage.'

Then I came to the treasure – Morecambe and Wise. 'They stayed
here?' I asked falteringly.

'Always stayed here, always had the same room,' came the reply.

'Can I see it?' I asked.

It was an ordinary digs room with two single beds, two little night
tables, a brown wood wardrobe and a double act of armchairs.

'Which bed did Eric sleep in?' I asked.

'I've no idea, love,' dismissed Mrs McKay.

'I'll take it,' I snapped.

She sensed something in the urgency of my voice. What she didn't
realize was that Eric was my hero; one of the great four who ruled the
world and were honoured with a picture on my bedroom wall. There was
Sean Connery as Bond, his sniper's eyes following you round the room.
Ursula Andress, dripping sex as she emerged from the Caribbean waves
as Honey Rider. Cassius Clay before he defied conscription, discovered
Allah and became Mohammed Ali. Then Eric, a middle-aged man
wearing his glasses at a bizarre angle. In the darkest days of my youth
they were the four who came to my rescue – Clay with his shuffle, Bond
with his Walther PPK, Honey Rider with her saltwater kisses and, finally,
Eric wearing a surprised look and an unfeasibly large pair of trousers.

There was something about the place that smelt old and tired. I took the room, paid double, didn't care. I knew I didn't have long, as I was only in town for twenty-four hours. I got into bed, took out my alarm clock and set it for 3 a.m. Hours later, when the alarm went off, I prised myself out of the warm sheets, crossed the room and climbed into the other bed. It was cold and I couldn't sleep, so I lay there playing Eric and Ernie over and over in my head – Eric making model aeroplanes in the flat, Ernie's meanness, the guest stars, the Christmas Day thrill of watching these two idiots side by side in their sexless bedroom, Ernie staring in blank incomprehension at the *Financial Times*, while Eric revelled in the *Beano*. I laughed myself to sleep.

Next day, I stood in front of a microphone, still nervous, still new, but with a secret. No one could touch me; I'd slept part of the night in Eric Morecambe's bed.

memories of eric

# James Dreyfus

Actor James Dreyfus shot to prominence in the Rowan Atkinson sit-com *The Thin Blue Line*. He also starred in the film *Boyfriends* and, more recently, with Kathy Burke in the outrageous BBC2 sit-com *Gimme, Gimme, Gimme*.

I was fascinated by Eric. No matter what he did, no matter what he said, no matter what facial expression he made, it was always spot-on. His humour and humanity always used to shine through and his comedic sense of life infected every part of my being. I remember at the age of thirteen, sitting in front of the TV crying with laughter at the fact that he, too, was laughing when he shouldn't have been and that, above all, made me laugh all the more. He gave me all the best lessons in comedy. Eric Morecambe has influenced every single comedian in this country since his death. If anyone disputes that, they are lying.

# Ben Elton

Writer and comedian Ben Elton is another lifelong
fan of Morecambe and Wise.

The only rule of comedy is honesty. Some say it's timing,
but it isn't. Timing's obviously important, but it has more
to do with understanding the right moment. Honesty is belief
in what you're doing. Whether you're doing something which
is based on a fairly complex idea, like I do, or you're doing a
piece of work based solely on your own exuberance, such as
Eric coughing 'Arsenal', you've really got to believe in it;
really got to know it's funny.

And you just knew that Eric believed in that act. He
believed in it so much, it ceased to become an act as such.

Sometimes the bickering in a double act is wooden – but
Morecambe and Wise were never wooden. If Eric's talent had
been playwriting or classical acting, he'd have been knighted.
In a different discipline, he would have been studied at
universities. That was the level of his achievement and his
honesty.

But there's nothing duller than discussing a joke or
analysing comedy. I mean, how can one really define a man
who could make you weep with laughter simply by coughing
the word 'Arsenal'?

I can honestly say Morecambe and Wise were my
favourite act of all time, and I like to think Eric was every bit
as nice, and perhaps just a little flawed, as he was on screen.

Eric on Eric

I was born quite young, and my real name is Eric Bartholomew. I adopted the name of my home town for the simple reason that you couldn't call me Eric Blackpool, could you?

My most special memory of Morecambe is the day the whole town came to see me off – and told me never to come back.

☆

I think I was popular with my teachers. Not on weekdays, though. Only Saturdays and Sundays.

■ (Gary: In fact, Eric loved his home town. In 1976 he wrote, 'My kind of town. That's Morecambe. It has to be for, like a badge, I carry the town with me. When I joined up with one Ernest Wiseman over thirty years ago, he shortened his name and I changed mine. Bartholomew didn't seem to fit the music-hall bills, so I replaced it with the town of my birth. Over the years, I reckon I've been a one-man public relations office for Morecambe. In fact, I think the council should raise a halfpenny rate in my favour for services rendered....My memories of my home town are serene and ageless. They emerge vivid and sharp. Happy and bright, not dull and ugly. For in those golden growing-up years, there was a sort of magic about Morecambe. It had a lot to offer and I took it. And during the years of travel that followed in my nomadic profession, much of that magic remained. It still does.')

People often ask me about wearing spectacles, and how I make use of them in our act, and whether I really need them. I'd like to get this business cleared up. I wear them only to see with – without glasses I couldn't even hear!

☆

When the war was on, I went down the mines as a Bevin Boy. My height was no handicap, as I worked lying down. Happy days? Yes, the days were very happy indeed – I was working nights.

☆

It's funny how things change as you get older. I first met up with Ernie Wise when we were thirteen-year-olds doing turns on *Youth Takes a Bow*. I remember what I thought of him then. The only word for it was 'strange'. But now I know him so much better I've changed that. He's 'very strange'.

☆

Apart from wartime, I've spent most of my life in show business, but there was a memorable three months when I worked in a razor-blade factory in Morecambe. I'm the only person who can hold up two fingers in a pub and get four beers!... It was about that time that I realized I could make people laugh. I held up four beers and was served two fingers – everybody laughed.

☆

Yes, I'll always remember the first big laugh I got professionally. I can also remember the last big laugh I got. It was the same one.

☆

Between you and me, I don't really mean all those insults I hurl at Des O'Connor. I think he's one of the greatest singers in the country. He just struggles when he sings in town, that's all. Have you heard his latest record, *Songs for Deaf Lovers*? There's a government health warning on every cover.

☆

People always ask me if Ernie really does wear a wig. I'm sworn to secrecy, but let's just say that he keeps Axminster Carpets in business. Without him, they'd be on the floor.

☆

Seriously, there's only one secret to a double act like ours: you've got to get on. And I can swear on the life of my kiddies we've never had a row. Not a real row. I mean, we disagree now and again over the way a joke should be done, but we've never had a row. He's such a nice feller – how can you dislike anyone like that?

I try not to think what I'd do if he wasn't around. I expect I'd take six months off, then try another show with another partner, another straight man. No, not exactly a straight man, because Ernie's not a straight man: like Tony Hancock had Sid James, someone like that... it wouldn't be another double act: it wouldn't be the Eric Morecambe–Charlie Smith Show. But I need a partner; on my own I just prattle on. Ernie senses this; he knows when I'm going off and he brings me down to earth with exactly the right line, and that's marvellous.

☆

Eric with his good friend, Dick Francis

All comedians are supposed to want to play Hamlet, I know, but that's not me. I was offered Bottom by the BBC a couple of weeks ago – the part of Bottom, that is – in *A Midsummer Night's Dream*. But I had to turn it down. I couldn't learn all those lines, for one thing.

# Postscript

On 9 May 1999, at the BAFTA awards ceremony, HRH the Princess Royal announced that Eric and Ernie had been awarded British Academy fellowships. Her words sum up well the affection and admiration so many people still feel for them.

Questions of quality and standards concern us all, and the British Academy celebrates television at the very highest standard. The fellowship is a very special occasion, and this year the Academy has decided to break with tradition and award a posthumous fellowship; in fact, two posthumous fellowships. I can think of no two people more deserving of this tribute than Morecambe and Wise: Eric and Ernie. It's a reminder of how very, very funny the two of them were and what enormous talent they had. They were, to use a well-worn phrase, a National Institution.

*Joan Morecambe and Doreen Wise with Des O'Connor at the BAFTA Awards ceremony*

# Eric Morecambe: A Chronology

1926 Born John Eric Bartholomew, 14 May. Only child of George and Sadie Bartholomew.

1936 Joins his cousin Peggy at Miss Hunter's dancing-school in Morecambe. Joins his fellow dancing-pupils in entertaining OAPs at church functions; does a song-and-dance double act with local girl, Molly Bunting.

1938 Leaves school aged twelve to pursue a career in show business.

1939 Wins talent competition organized by *Melody Maker*; auditions for Jack Hylton in Manchester, where he meets Ernie Wise for the first time.

1941 Eric and Ernie appear as a double act for the first time (Liverpool Empire). Eric adopts the name Morecambe.

1943 Appears with Ernie in smash-hit show *Strike a New Note*. First radio appearance in *Youth Must Have its Fling*.

1944 Called up and sent down the mines in Accrington as a Bevin Boy.

1945 Invalided out of the mines with poor health and minor heart trouble.

1946 Resumes double act with Ernie.

1947 Tours with Ernie in Lord John Sanger's Circus and Variety Tour.

1950 Morecambe and Wise sign with agent Frank Pope and begin appearing regularly in Moss Empire Theatres, the leading variety theatres.

1952 Marries Joan Bartlett, 11 December.

1953 Daughter, Gail, is born. Morecambe and Wise have their own radio series, *You're Only Young Once*.

1954 Morecambe and Wise's first – and unsuccessful – series for BBC TV, *Running Wild*.

1956 Son Gary born. Buy first house in North Finchley, London. Morecambe and Wise resume TV career, appearing with Winifred Atwell on ITV with scripts written by Johnny Speight.

1958 Morecambe and Wise tour Australia.

1960 Morecambe and Wise join the agent Billy Marsh.

1961 Morecambe and Wise's ATV series begins. Eric and Ernie invited to appear on the Royal Command Performance.

1961 Eric moves with his family to Harpenden, Hertfordshire.

1963 Morecambe and Wise win their first of six BAFTAS

1964 The Beatles are guest stars on *The Morecambe and Wise Show*. Morecambe and Wise make their first appearance on *The Ed Sullivan Show* for CBS. First film, *The Intelligence Men*, filmed at at Pinewood Studios. Honoured by Variety Club.

1965 *That Riviera Touch* filmed at Pinewood.

1966 *The Magnificent Two* filmed at Pinewood.

1968 Morecambe and Wise smash all records in summer season at Great Yarmouth and leave ATV to join BBC TV. November, Eric suffers first heart attack.

1969 Resumes performing. Eddie Braben begins writing scripts for Morecambe and Wise. Wins BAFTA award.

1970 Voted Pipe-Smoker of the Year. Becomes director of Luton Town Football Club. Wins BAFTA award.

1971 André Previn, Shirley Bassey and Glenda Jackson all make highly publicized debuts on *The Morecambe and Wise Show*.

Wins BAFTA award and is honoured by the Radio Industries Organization.

1972 BAFTA award.

1973 Profiled by Kenneth Tynan in the *Observer Magazine*. BAFTA award. Morecambe and Wise publish joint autobiography, *Eric and Ernie*.

1974 Adopts son Steven. Honoured by Variety Club and Water Rats.

1976 Awarded the OBE, the Freedom of the City of London and an honorary degree by the University of Lancaster. Father, George Bartholomew, dies. Honoured by Variety Club.

1977 Mother, Sadie Bartholomew, dies. Becomes president of the Lord's Taverners. *The Morecambe and Wise Show* is watched by a record 28 million viewers.

1978 Morecambe and Wise join Thames Television. Former prime minister Harold Wilson is guest star on first Christmas show. Variety Club award.

1979 Suffers second heart attack and subsequently undergoes pioneering bypass surgery. Appears in short film for Anglia TV based on works by John Betjeman.

1980 Writes first novel, *Mr Lonely*, while recovering from bypass surgery. Appears in second short Betjeman film for Anglia TV. 1981 *Mr Lonely* published to critical acclaim. Morecambe and Wise voted into TV Hall of Fame.

1982 Writes *The Reluctant Vampire*, a novel for children.

1983 Writes *The Vampire's Revenge*, a novel for children.

1984 Writes *Eric Morecambe on Fishing*. Completes *Night Train to Murder*, a film destined to be last work he does with Ernie Wise. Dies of third heart attack following a charity performance at the Roses Theatre, Tewkesbury, on 28 May.

1985 *Stella*, his second adult novel, completed by Gary Morecambe, published. *Morecambe and Wife*, by Joan Morecambe, published.

1987 *The Illustrated Morecambe*, by Gary Morecambe, published.

1990 *Still On My Way To Hollywood*, Ernie's autobiography, published.

1994 Biography *Morecambe and Wise:*

*Behind the Sunshine*, by Gary Morecambe and Martin Sterling, becomes a bestseller. A BBC compilation of classic Morecambe and Wise shows to mark the tenth anniversary of Eric's death, and hosted by Ben Elton, tops the ratings.

1995 Blue plaque commemorating Eric put up by Comic Heritage in London. Ernie announces retirement from show business aged 70.

1996 Morecambe and Wise voted the favourite entertainers of all time by television viewers' poll to mark sixty years of BBC Television.

1998 *Radio Times* readers vote Morecambe and Wise the best TV comedy stars of all time. *Morecambe and Wise*, by Graham McCann, published. *Omnibus: The Heart and Soul of Eric Morecambe* broadcast on BBC1.

1999 Ernie Wise dies, aged 73. Eric and Ernie each awarded a posthumous BAFTA fellowship. Statue of Eric unveiled by HM The Queen in Morecambe, Lancashire.

## PHOTO CREDITS